Bureau of Land Management

California

The Historic Archaeology Of A Chinese Mining Venture Near Igo In Northern California

By

Eric W. Ritter

Cultural Resources Report

Archaeology

THE HISTORIC ARCHAEOLOGY OF A CHINESE MINING
VENTURE NEAR IGO IN NORTHERN CALIFORNIA

Eric W. Ritter

Bureau of Land Management
Ukiah District
Redding Resource Area

Redding, California

1986

TABLE OF CONTENTS

LIST OF TABLES

LIST OF MAP AND FIGURES

ACKNOWLEDGMENTS

While the author takes the responsibility for this report, a number of individuals deserve credit for their assistance. Those who kindly reviewed a draft and offered helpful comments include Francis Berg, Jeff LaLande, Mary Maniery, Joe Molter, James Rock, Ron Rogers, Mary Rusco, Dana Seldner, Judy Tordoff and Priscilla Wegars. Pete Schulz provided faunal identifications. Gary Mullett, Norm Myers, Virgil Haven and Louis Wacker helped in the mapping and map preparations. Illustrations were capably prepared by Carol Farber, Patty Cook and Brenda Ault. Charlene Bailey and Beth Elstien assisted in the field. A difficult task amiably completed by Patty Cook was the word processing. To all these individuals and the Bureau of Land Management, which supported my work, I am most grateful.

INTRODUCTION

In 1980 it was stated that "It should be apparent that many more descriptive reports will be required, from different types of sites and different periods, before specific models can be formulated for either the frontier or urban Chinese experience" (Greenwood 1980:119). LaLande (1981:343) a year later noted "Chinese site archaeology may soon reach a point of redundancy in certain aspects of the material culture..." Felton et al. (1984:3) found that "Although we have witnessed a number of archaeological investigations of overseas-Chinese sites in recent years, many of these sites date to the 1880s and later, or have yielded only small collections." Greenway (1985:7) has commented on the obvious need for additional comparative studies of Chinese and Euro-American mining sites. Lastly, Smith (1983:11) has urged: "But as archaeology is strongly characterized by a synthetic and comparative orientation, the most useful delineations of cultural patterning are recognized as evolving out of the union of multiple studies directed toward common research questions."

These statements bear directly on the value of a limited archaeological project involving mapping and data recovery from several trash dumps, a reservoir, ditches and other features of a small historic rural Chinese mining operation (CA-Sha-1512) in the vicinity of Igo in Shasta County, California (Township 31 North, Range 6 West, Section 34) (Figure 1). This site was discovered during a routine survey of public land in response to a mining proposal. This archaeological project may deal with only part of a larger historic mining system or systems encompassing a goodly portion of southwestern Shasta County. Nevertheless, in conjunction with nearby regional studies of Chinese mining activities (Smith 1983; Johnson and Theodoratus 1984; Seldner, 1986; Tordoff 1986) an opportunity was presented to study archaeological remains related to Chinese use at one site and integrate the work into the broader examination. In this manner, history can be supplemented and corrected; anthropological inquiries made fruitful.

Certainly this project did not evolve through the ideal process of development of an explicit set of goals in order to generate field methods and analytical techniques. Rather, discovery of major features (a ditch system and dam) led to a program of mapping and evaluation through a comparative analysis. There were no obvious habitation or associated refuse areas. During the mapping phase a detailed examination of features led to the finding of several trash dumps with a high percentage of Chinese goods strongly suggesting Chinese association. Materials from these dumps and the general area were recovered as part of the mitigation process.

Following data gathering (and in tune with ongoing research of similar remains just miles away), the analysis and report herein were generated. This was bearing in mind the regional research goals of Chinese ethnohistory and archaeology of Johnson and Theodoratus (1984:375-380), the research issues of Smith (1983:9-11), and some new research questions presented below. Information exchange with the Dutch Gulch Lake researchers (cf. Tordoff 1986) was an important

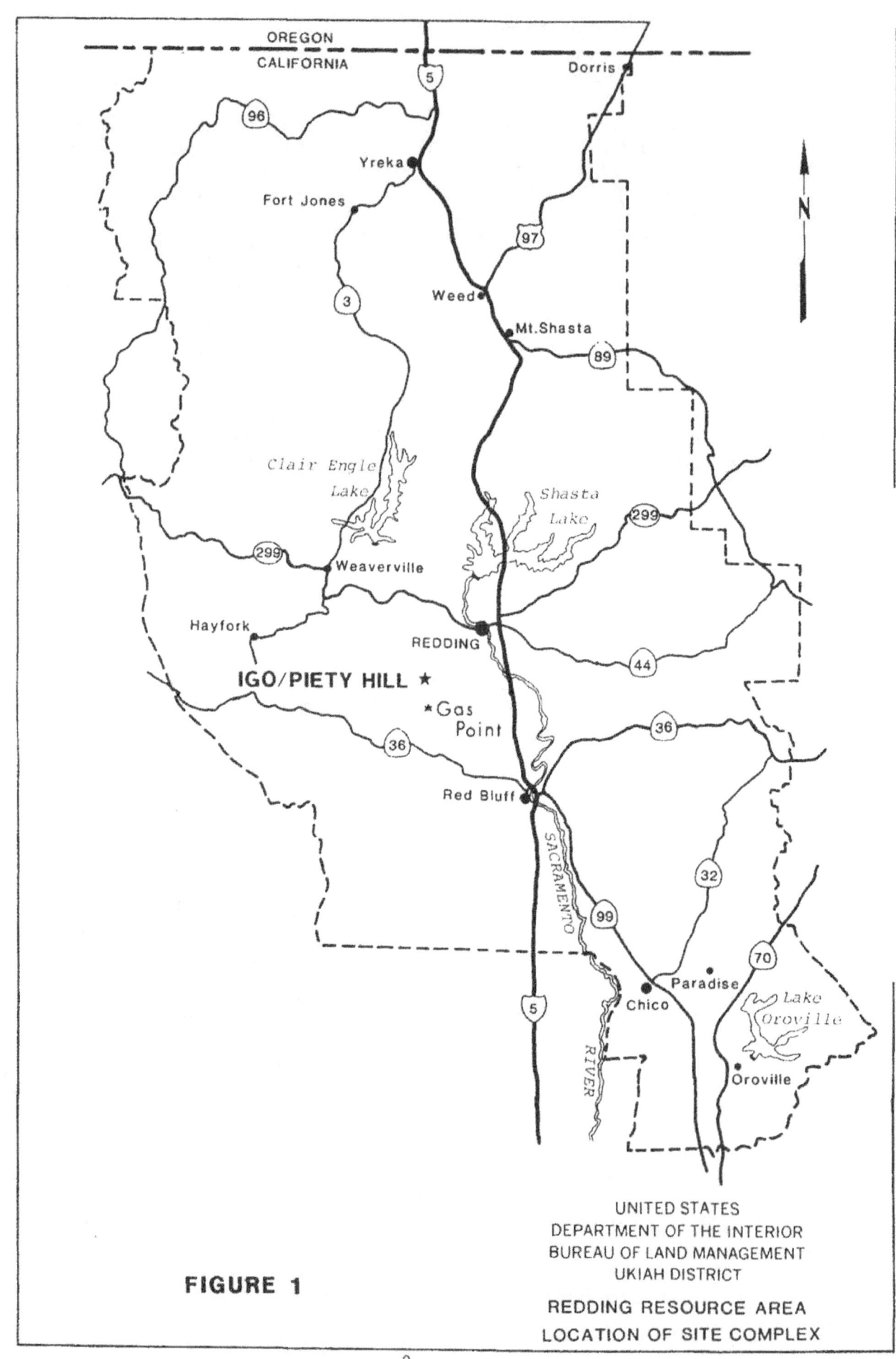

FIGURE 1

UNITED STATES
DEPARTMENT OF THE INTERIOR
BUREAU OF LAND MANAGEMENT
UKIAH DISTRICT

REDDING RESOURCE AREA
LOCATION OF SITE COMPLEX

facet of the study and, as stated, this research should be viewed in concert with the larger nearby work. The avenues taken in this work can hopefully alleviate some of the concerns stated by Greenwood (1980), LaLande (1981), Smith (1983), perhaps implied by Felton et al. (1984), as well as the plea from Greenway (1985).

Principal research questions thought relevant to this study (aside from chronological questions) and through which model development of historic rural Chinese mining ventures can be formulated, are summarized as follows:

Settlement/Economics/Social Interaction

1. How can historic Euro-American and Chinese settlement and activity areas be distinguished, especially with regard to gold mining, and was there any cross-fertilization of mining practices, as in ditch and reservoir construction?

2. How did historic Chinese mining operations and ancillary activities vary regionally over time and how do these activities relate to broader patterns or practices of Chinese mining, economics and social relations in differing regions and areas?

3. What was the nature of historic Chinese subsistence and technology in the vicinity and region?

4. What influence did Euro-American commerce have on Chinese commerce within this region, and vice-versa? For instance, what use did the Chinese make of Anglo stores?

5. What were the social and economic relationships between the local Chinese miners and their Euro-American counterparts, and what effects, if any, did these relationships have on activities over the land and through time? Is there any suggestion of racial prejudice on the part of local Anglos?

6. What was the interaction between the local (rural) historic Chinese and those in urban settings, and how did these interactions vary over time? Was there an established commercial network?

7. What relationship, if any, exists between resource competition, racial bias and/or social organization of the historic Chinese miners and other groups with regard to settlement/activity patterning over the land?

Mining Operations

8. How were Chinese activities at the site area manifested seasonally, especially as they relate to mining oriented behavior?

9. What differences exist between Chinese mining and settlement activities at Igo, Dutch Gulch and other areas as the distance and transportation costs increase from centers of commerce with Chinese populations?

10. How do the Igo/Dutch Gulch Chinese mining activities compare or contrast with those Euro-American mining endeavors of the same era in the same mining province and those elsewhere in California, and what factors, such as water availability, presence of lodes, etc., influence the variability?

11. What are the relationships between historic Chinese mining techniques within the region and homeland water control practices, as in irrigation?

12. What relationship exists between the gold productivity of historic Chinese workings and those of surrounding Euro-American miners, and what factors, such as labor intensity, influence the difference, if present or definable?

Site Structure/Patterning

13. Does the Igo Chinese mining site represent a single company's efforts, part of one company's efforts, or some other combination?

14. How were the mining area's associated activity/habitation loci structured? Were certain activities concentrated or dispersed? What are the underlying factors (such as proximity to nearby Chinese communities) to the site structuring and activity patterning? How does the structuring and patterning relate to the regional Chinese pattern?

Assimilation/Acculturation

15. What influences were rendered by Euro-American culture on the Chinese occupant/users with regard to mining and non-mining-related technology, and subsistence, leisure activities and other cultural aspects?

16. Where non-traditional technology and goods were utilized, is this use a reflection of newly homogenized preferences and cognitive changes requisite for "true" acculturation, or just temporary acquisitions necessitated by limited access?

17. If acculturation of historic Chinese miners can be determined, how does this fit with the "Sojourner Thesis" (Lee 1960) or the "Ethnic Constraint Theory" (Rusco and Hattori 1986)?

18. If there is no indication of acculturation or assimilation, how is this reconciled with a locally declining population and perhaps more limited access to Chinese goods, services and/or social networks? For example, was the Exclusion Act locally influential?

4

19. With declining Chinese populations and limitations on certain mining practices, did mining activities become more individualistic and smaller in scale?

These and other questions will be addressed through the feature and artifactual analyses, archival study, comparative work and discussion to follow.

LOCAL ENVIRONMENTAL BACKGROUND

The Igo area of Shasta County lies within the Klamath Mountains geologic province of northern California. Specifically, the western Sacramento Valley foothills surrounding the site are largely Pleistocene alluvial deposits of the Red Bluff formation, ancient Sacramento River terraces and filled channels overlying volcanic beds of the Tuscan Formation. These terraces are dissected by Dry Creek, a perennial stream (in segments), which flows easterly into Cottonwood Creek, a major tributary of the Sacramento River. The site complex is located on the main terrace tread 500 feet north of Dry Creek. Just over a mile to the northeast is Clear Creek, the location of the earliest gold mining ventures in the county. The town of Igo is located on the divide between the Clear Creek and Cottonwood Creek drainage systems (see Appendix 1).

The soil in the site vicinity is a Newtown gravelly loam (Klaseen and Ellison 1974:Sheet 87). This is a deep, well-drained soil which supports a mixed oak woodland and chaparral community consisting predominantly of oaks and Digger pine, manzanita, and various grasses and forbs. Patches of dense manzanita cover portions of the site. A fuller discussion of the general environmental setting is provided in Johnson and Theodoratus (1984:4-7).

HISTORIC BACKGROUND

Mining ventures in the vicinity of Igo/Piety Hill commenced in earnest about 1851 with the establishment of the Soft Scrabble Mine by William Forschler (Ballou 1954:19). Subsequently, an ancient river channel and gravels were discovered cutting across the ridge between Clear Creek and Dry Creek leading to the establishment of the town of Piety Hill and the Hardscrabble Mine, and the working of deposits nearby including those in the immediate vicinity of CA-Sha-1512 or what the author has designated as the "Igo Chinese Workings", the focus of this report.

The Hardscrabble Mine was organized into the Dry Creek Tunnel and Fluming Company with Bob Harvey and George F. McPherson, superintendents. Historic land plats from the General Land Office of 1857 show roads heading in the direction of the site area from Igo/Piety Hill, but no other features (see Appendix 1). The township plat of 1875 illustrates the Piety Hill Placer Mine to the east and north and the Igo Lost Channel Mines Consolidated Placer Mine to the south and partly on the west of the 40 acres of isolated public land on which the operation under study is located (Appendix 1). Other property to the west is not listed by name on this plat. However, as discussed in this section, the mineral plats are more revealing.

William K. Conger on April 5, 1852 filed a water right application with the County (County of Shasta, Records Book B, page 70) for the purpose of diverting water to Dry Creek. In the application it is noted that a race or races were to be built "leading to adjacent flats for the purpose of washing the dirt within flats or gulches." Seven years later on November 14, 1859, I. F. Stanley claimed all water in Dry Creek for mining purposes (County of Shasta, Record Book S, page 111).

As the need for water and water control increased in the 1860s with the expanding mining enterprises and population, a corresponding but perhaps unrelated influx of Chinese into the site area began. Increased numbers apparently followed a decline in regional Chinese populations around 1855 upon the heels of an anti-Chinese resolution drawn up by white miners (Chiu 1963:19). Johnson and Theodoratus (1984:256) note that a few Chinese had settled in the area by 1860. Giles (1949:151) indicates that according to the 1852 census there were 2,000 to 3,000 Chinese in Shasta County, although the number around Igo was probably small. Still, Blandin (1971:62), in reference to the general area of Igo, notes that "In 1851 the Chinese dug a twenty-mile ditch to convey water from enough small streams to build up pressure for hydraulic mining." Andrews (1964:15) states that in the area the labor for digging the ditches was mostly done by Chinese. Peterson (1965:92) indicates that the Hardscrabble Mine reportedly used 600 Chinese in the 1860s for flume and ditch construction bringing water from the North Fork of Cottonwood Creek to the Igo vicinity. Andrews (1964:15) says, "About four hundred of them (Chinese) came to Piety Hill diggings and helped in the great expansion that was taking place then; they also engaged in mining on their own behalf by learning from white men." Ballou (1954:19) indicates that about 600 Chinese were located at Piety Hill about this time, and it would seem that the Chinese population in the Piety Hill vicinity considerably expanded in the 1860s from earlier levels.

Apparently, a number of Chinese individuals or small companies were not content with helping Euro-American enterprises and evidently they began to accumulate capital and, sometimes, expand or form new operations. On June 19, 1866, Ah Choy & Co. purchased the water rights of John Wheelock near Igo along the North Fork of Cottonwood Creek, including ditches on both sides of the creek, a precursor to extensive mining (County of Shasta, Record Book S, page 468). Chiu (1963:31) notes that for California "The bulk of the Chinese mining companies in this period 1865-1880, employed 15-20 workers, owned a claim of two to three thousand dollars, exclusive of equipment, and engaged in hydraulic or drift mining." In this regard, Johnson and Theodoratus' (1984:266) statement that "...unlike the case in 1880...Chinese miners tended to work in small groups in 1870. This seems to suggest a lesser degree of organization than in later years" should be considered further. Judith Tordoff of California State University, Sacramento (personal communication 1986) feels this is more a result of population increase than organization. By 1856 in nearby Trinity County there were Chinese companies all along the Trinity River (Hanover 1982:14-15). However, Hanover mentions that a company could be as small as two, three, or four people (1982:12).

The immediate area of the "Igo Chinese Workings" does not appear to have any such record for Chinese activities during the era of large-scale hydraulic mining (1865-1890) until near the era's end as subsequently discussed (cf. Johnson and Theodoratus 1984:265). However, as previously mentioned, there is documentation for mining and mining-related activities where the Chinese were often employed elsewhere in the region (within several miles and beyond).

George McPherson and others on behalf of the Dry Creek Tunnel and Fluming Company (apparently at that time called the Shasta Hydraulic Mining Company--or at least they were associated) applied for water rights from the North Fork of Cottonwood Creek and Jerusalem Creek in 1868 and 1871 (County of Shasta, Record Book S, pages 501 and 521), with water to be diverted in the Ed Jones Ditch and the Dry Creek Tunnel and Fluming Company Ditch, respectively. Then, in 1874 (County of Shasta, Miscellaneous Records Book 1, page 150) more water from the North Fork of Cottonwood Creek was acquired by right.

Water in 1872 (County of Shasta, Miscellaneous Records Book 1, page 82) was acquired from Dry Creek for the "purpose of working the dirt and gravel from the bed of Dry Creek through the tunnel of the Dry Creek Tunnel and Fluming Company...by means of a ditch 3 feet deep, 4 feet wide on the bottom and 6 feet wide at the top."

During operation of the Hardscrabble Mine, various transactions were officially recorded with the County. For example, there is the sale of some claims of the Hardscrabble group by George McPherson and others to the Shasta Mining Company on October 8, 1868 (County of Shasta, Deeds Book 3, pages 119-120). What is particularly relevant here is reference to one claim near Conger Gulch "just across the reservoir", apparent reference to the large reservoir in the site vicinity discussed later.

On December 12, 1870, a 2/5th interest in the Cottonwood (or Jones) Ditch and Dry Creek Tunnel and Fluming Company was given by George McPherson and John Skinner to B. G. Lathrop who was to furnish hydraulic apparatus and operation funds (County of Shasta, Agreements Book 1, pages 2-3).

The town of Piety Hill was found to be situated in the path of ongoing hydraulic operations in association with the Hardscrabble Mine. As such, Superintendent McPherson in 1866 laid out a new townsite across Conger Gulch on ground determined to be unproductive. Some houses were moved here from Piety Hill. This town was named Igo (Ballou 1954:20) and remains to this day.

In 1884 a federal court order outlawed hydraulic mining in the Sacramento Valley drainage system without proper debris control, although this order was difficult to enforce (cf. Bente and Smith 1984). This date corresponds with the closing of the Dry Creek Tunnel and Fluming Company's extensive operation and the sale of the big ditch and 1700 acres of land to Alonzo Hayward for over half a million dollars (Andrews 1964:17). However, this clearly was not the end of mining operations in the area, nor of smaller-scale hydraulic operations.

According to Ballou (1954:20), the Chinese continued to live at Piety Hill long after the Euro-Americans left for Igo and elsewhere. There was a store run by a man called Can, vegetable gardens, duck pens, and a large brick oven and stove. According to Giles (1949:192), by 1888 it was wholly a Chinese town. Blandin (1971:62) relates a description of "the Chinese shacks in Piety Hill made of wood with little trails between rooms where the men would lie around smoking long pipes."

The report of the State Mineralogist (1892:336) indicates that "In the Igo and Ono Districts...there has been much work done during the past year." The subsequent report of 1894 provides the best information on late nineteenth century mining in the vicinity with a crucial passage relevant to the workings under prime consideration here, discussed below.

The Blue Bird Mine, listed as a drift mine (Report of the State Mineralogist 1894:246) is described as a 20-acre operation one-half mile south of Igo owned by Tom White. "The Dry Creek Water Company furnishes the water. Only a few boxes are used for washing, which are cleaned up monthly." It seems likely that the same ditch system that fed the "Igo Chinese Workings" provided water here as further related later. Even more convincing, it is likely that the Tom White listed here is the same Thomas White noted on the 1875 mineral plat for the adjoining Piety Hill Placer Mine (surveyed in 1873 and claimed by the Dry Creek Tunnel and Fluming Company) (Appendix 1) as owner of the westerly portion of the present public land piece. Ballou (1964:16) notes that "The Thomas White gravel mine on Dry Creek was a good producer, though the operation was small. It was reported to have yielded $150,000 in placer gold." The other portion of the public land piece appears to fall within the Piety Hill Placer Mine claim, although it is difficult to reconcile the early plat and recent maps. If so, then this portion of the claim may have later become Chinese controlled, as will be discussed shortly.

The Doebleine claim two miles east of Igo, comprising 200 acres, is listed as a hydraulic mine (Report of the State Mineralogist 1894:247). It is noted that:

> Water is caught in reservoirs and brought to the claim through 6 miles of ditch, using 2,000 foot of 8 inch pipe and a giant with 1 inch nozzle, under 100 foot pressure. For washing, 200 inches of water are used, and 20 boxes paved with block riffles.

This statement, while not describing the site under study, is probably a close approximation of the activities there (see Appendix 1).

In this same report the Hardscrabble Mine is discussed. The hydraulic mine is listed as composing 1,720 acres. Twenty-five acres are noted as having been worked. "Haber and Eagle Creeks and South Fork of Clear Creek furnish the water through 25 miles of main ditch, which carries 1,300 inches of water. The property is idle at present, not having placed any restraining dams for the debris" (Report of the State Mineralogist 1894:249). The Merchants Exchange Bank of San Fransisco is listed as the owner.

Another mine description in this report provides a revealing description of local activities and features possibly relevant to the "Igo Chinese Workings" (Report of the State Mineralogist 1894:255). The Red Hill hydraulic mine near Ono is listed as comprising 60 acres. The gravel bank in this case was loosened with high explosives, with processing water provided by Dry Creek Tunnel and Fluming Company's ditch. The mine is listed as using 100 inches of water, under 50 foot of pressure, brought through 1-1/4 miles of ditch. Particularly revealing is the statement that the water season lasts ten months, suggesting nearly year-round mining activities. However, it is noted that 500 inches of water could be obtained for four months of the year, and 100 inches for six months by digging the necessary ditches. Debris dams are listed as five brush and one stone dam.

The location and discussion of the Schuyler mine, three-fourths of a mile from Igo (Report of the State Mineralogist 1894:256-257), most closely fits the "Igo Chinese Workings" or CA-Sha-1512. This mine is designated as both drift and hydraulic. A tunnel 1,900 feet long is listed with three air shafts 48 to 66 foot in depth.

"The hydraulic portion of the claim has a 55 foot bank, washed with 75 foot of water pressure, and uses twenty-two foot sluice boxes set on a 5 inch grade, and paved with block riffles. There are two brush restraining dams and one stone dam on Dry Creek for the debris."

Most significantly, a "Chinese Company" is listed as the owner, probably a successor to Thomas White and possibly part of the Piety Hill mine. The subsequent Report of the State Mineralogist (1896:364) notes that a Chinese Company was still the owner but that the mine was idle. The presence of Chinese artifacts at this site (as discussed in this report) certainly seems to coincide with the expected pattern considering the listed owners.

Chinese mining ventures in the region (at Gas Point 3-5 miles south) continued for several years after this reported operation. An agreement between Wing Yuen and Company of San Francisco (Joe Foo, Agent) and Frank and Maria Henriquez was reached on March 10, 1899 for use of a ditch on the Henriquez property in return for some water from the ditch for irrigation. The Chinese company claimed to be involved in cleaning out and enlarging the ditch and wished to do this and some new construction on the Henriquez property. They also stated they were in the process of negotiating from a third party for lands to form a continuum of property, apparently along the route of the ditch (County of Shasta, Agreement Book 3, pages 472-473). It seems very unlikely considering the terrain and scope of work that this operation was for agricultural purposes. This is the last entry regarding Chinese mining ventures in the area, although later Chinese mining activities in northern California have been documented (cf. Clark 1963:135). Chinese mining companies continued to work on the Trinity River at this time as well.

The U.S. Census of 1900 for the Igo township lists a number of Chinese residents, four at least who appear to have been residing in Igo (or Piety Hill). These latter individuals (Guen Ah, Twoy Ah, Can Ah and Bok Giu) all owned their houses outright. These individuals (designated aliens) had been residing in the United States for 20 or 30 years, having arrived during the hydraulic mining boom. Guen Ah and his wife Twoy arrived from Canton in 1880 at the age of 21 and 20 respectively and list both their occupations as placer miners. They are listed as speaking and writing English, and employed. They also list no children. Bok Giu, a single male born in 1824, came to the United States from Canton in 1870 at the age of 46. He also lists his occupation as placer miner. He neither spoke nor wrote in English. Can Ah, undoubtedly the storekeeper Can remembered by Ballou (1954:20), and listed in the census as storekeeper, was born in 1832, arriving in California in 1870, at age 38. He is noted as married and literate in English, but no wife is listed. Several other Chinese residents of the township are registered as placer miners, also arriving since 1870 from Canton.

Euro-American mining operations in the Dry Creek vicinity continued at this same time. Henry Chapman and John Lowden in 1899 applied for water rights from Dry Creek for running hydraulic equipment (County of Shasta, Water Rights Book 1899, page 98). J. M. Rust and C. A. Russell applied for water rights on Dry Creek at the mouth of Condor (Conger?) Creek for mining and milling of the lost channel claims utilizing a ditch 5 feet wide at the top, 3 feet wide at the bottom, and 2 feet deep (County of Shasta, Water Rights Book 1909, page 208). The Searchlight (1898) of Redding reported that "There is considerable surface mining by individuals in the vicinity of Igo."

Mining in the local area continued off and on to the present. For example, the Igo Lost Channel Mines Consolidated Placer just to the south was not patented until 1950 (Mineral Survey Plat No. 6466, Bureau of Land Management, Sacramento). There has been renewed interest in mining the public land by the Igo Gold Placer Company, owner, of Agoura Hills, California under the operation of Consolidated Placer Dredging, Inc. of San Francisco who filed a notice of intent for mining with the Bureau of Land Management in June of 1984. It is important to note that in their notice they refer to the large area along Dry Creek of past mining characterized by tailings, roads and the bluff itself as the "China Pit". The derivation of this term is uncertain, but probably relates to the Chinese operations discussed previously.

During the historic period the Igo region was dominated by gold mining activities, beginning very shortly after Marshall's discovery along the American River. There has also been a local Chinese presence, acting individually and in a group structure, under Euro-American, local Chinese or distant (e.g. San Francisco) Chinese corporations.

This background serves as context within which to evaluate the archaeological remains discovered. Together they form the basis for the inferences and conclusions that follow.

FIELD METHODOLOGY

The site complex was originally found during a routine archaeological survey. Initially, a dam and reservoir area and a few scattered artifacts were recorded. Subsequent visits, especially during the mapping phase, led to a better definition of various features.

Mapping of the dam/reservoir and associated features was accomplished through use of a Hewlett-Packard Model 3810 A Electronic Distance Meter. Some of the smaller features were mapped with a hand compass and tape measure (Map 1).

Two adjoining dumps were identified during the mapping phase. These proved to contain the majority of the artifacts recovered. Materials within these dumps occurred on the surface or within a thin duff layer, sometimes imbedded within the underlying soil. No artifacts occurred more than two inches (5 cm) below the surface. Trowel and McLeod fire tool excavation into the subsoil of these two dumps proved negative. Each dump area was treated as a recovery unit due to its relative localized nature. However, attention was paid in the larger (southerly) dump to those materials from the easterly and westerly halves. Artifacts were not individually plotted.

Each dump was scraped systematically into a series of piles from one edge to the other, section by section, using the tools mentioned, and except for the easterly half of the larger dump, screened through 1/4" mesh shaker screens. The easterly portion of the larger dump was scraped with a trowel and the matrix carefully examined by eye. Several sorts were made of the loosened material in the search for artifacts.

In addition to the above, the complex was walked over a number of times with encountered artifacts recorded or collected for study.

Map 1

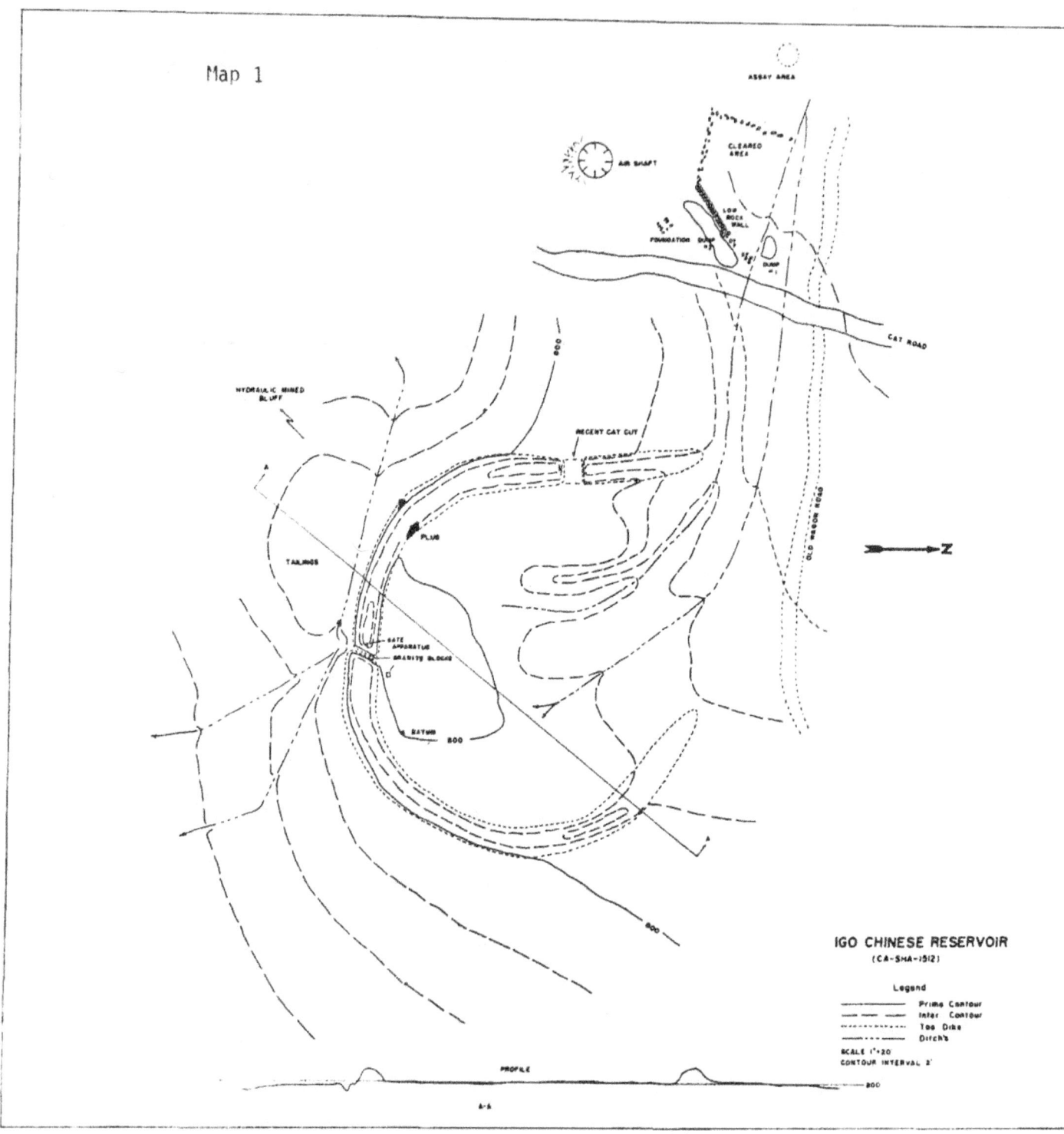

IGO CHINESE RESERVOIR
(CA-SHA-1512)

Legend

Prime Contour	
Inter Contour	
Toe Dike	
Ditch's	

SCALE 1"=20'
CONTOUR INTERVAL 2'

14

FEATURES

The focus of the regional mining operations was the auriferous Pleistocene gravels within the dissected hills between Clear and Dry creeks and erosional detritus. Throughout the historic mining period (circa 1850 to 1910) various operators and operations created a melange of features and debris. Aside from periodic recent activities related to renewed mining, grazing, and settlement, these features have remained undisturbed for archaeological study. The focus of this study is on a set of related features within one area of the Igo District.

Clearly the central feature to site operations (at least post 1880 or so) was an earthen berm reservoir and its associated ditch system, both feeder and exit (Figs. 16a-c, 17a, b).

Dam-Reservoir

The berm or dam forming the reservoir is horseshoe shaped with a gate to the south in the center (Fig. 17a-c). The berm is 290 feet (88 m) long, six feet (2 m) wide at the base and two feet (0.6 m) at the top, and nearly seven feet (2.2 m) high at its outlet, with the berm tapering in height toward the ends. Utilizing a 25% compaction factor and estimating that siltation within the reservoir (and along the berm sides) has now exceeded one foot (30 cm) (judging from a bulldozer cut) then the dam is composed of about 270 cubic yards (226 cubic meters) of earthen material apparently removed from the reservoir area. One side of the earthen berm exhibits on the interior near the base a cobble and earthen plug, apparently an earlier outlet (Fig. 17b).

The reservoir formed by the initial construction is about 0.65 acres (0.26 hectares) in size with a holding capacity of approximately 2.0 acre feet (0.81 square hectares) of water. Such a size compares with the largest dams and reservoirs reported by Johnson and Theodoratus (1984:67) for Chinese miners in the nearby Dutch Gulch Lake project area several miles to the south and with the Chinese Diggings Reservoir at Malakoff Diggings in Nevada County (Felton et al., 1979:134). However, none compares with the considerably larger, seemingly related berm-reservoir system about 1/2 mile (650m) to the north-northeast along Cloverdale Road, which is some 10 to 15 times larger. Oak trees growing within the berm and the similarity of construction suggest relative contemporaneity of the features on Cloverdale Road and at CA-Sha-1512.

LaLande and Handschug (1983:6) report on a different trapezoidal form of Chinese-related dam fitting a small canyon in Jackson County, Oregon that they have labeled the Flumet Gulch Dam/Reservoir. This dam includes 3,000 cubic yards of material.

Ditches

These reservoir features near Igo were fed by a network of earthen ditches, emanating from streams up country (Fig. 17a). These ditches are discussed above in the background sections. In turn, ditches run from the reservoir outlets toward placered and hydraulicked hillsides beginning immediately to the south (Fig. 17c).

The feeder ditch to the reservoir at CA-Sha-1512 was traced to the town of Igo itself, where it is obliterated. Judging from aerial photos, it would appear to originate from the South Fork of Clear Creek or some of the tributary streams of Cottonwood Creek north of Ono. A separate ditch system, probably also from the South Fork of Clear Creek, fed the larger nearby reservoir.

The ditch feeding the smaller reservoir under consideration here diverges some 100 feet (30 m) and again about 500 feet (155 m) up-ditch where the branch to the reservoir has been plugged with earth and cobbles. The last used segment runs westerly to an area of mining along Placer Road about 1/2 mile (800 m) to the west of the reservoir complex. These workings may be the Blue Bird Mine discussed in the background section. The ditch measures about 6-8 feet (2-2.5 m) across by 2-3 feet (1 m) deep on the average with clear berms in most areas. In cross-section, the ditch is almost V-shaped with a flattened bottom, although some segments form more of an arc in cross-section perhaps in part due to erosion and deposition. The grade of the ditch is in the vicinity of one inch to the rod.

At the reservoir outlet there are three short ditches diverging amongst placered deposits. One ditch runs west and then south to a hydraulically mined bluff. The ditch appears to have been truncated by later (historic) mining activities.

Dumps

Along opposite sides of the feeder ditch, about 120 feet (37 m) west of the dam/reservoir, are two trash dumps, one quite small. These dumps are situated within small depressions, probably derived from earlier placer mining (Fig. 18b). The smaller northerly dump measures about 10 feet (3 m) by four feet (1.2 m) and consisted of one Chinese ceramic vessel, a liquor bottle and several metal artifacts. The larger, south dump measures about 45 feet (13.7 m) by 10 feet (3 m) and contained a number of Chinese and Euro-American ceramics, liquor bottles and household jars, nails, window glass, and numerous metal items, all discussed in the artifact section. Also within this dump were areas of ash and small pieces of charcoal probably indicative of fireplace cleanout since only one or two artifacts exhibit burning.

The small northerly dump would appear to represent a single event while the larger, or south dump probably relates to a number of events. One reason for this suggestion is the scattered and segregated nature of the materials at the large dump, as opposed to being one limited, homogenous pile. In the westerly portion of the south dump occurred many more nails, and all the wire nails; the majority of the vitrified white earthenware vessels, and the majority of the four flowers serving bowls. The easterly portion of the dump contained the four flowers dishes, a majority of brownware ceramics, the window glass and the few faunal remains. There is the

16

suggestion, based on the fragmented nature of some of the durable artifacts, that the large dump represents clean-up of broken material from a given area or areas with some artifact portions left or deposited elsewhere. The hidden nature of these dumps (within manzanita thickets under duff cover) suggests there could be others at this complex.

Cobble Alignments

Separate cobble alignment features occur on each side of the south or main dump. To the south is a low, one course high rectangular alignment of cobbles, perhaps a structure foundation or hearth area (Figure 18a). This alignment (unexcavated) measures at least eight feet (2.4 m) by five feet (1.5 m). Square cut nails and other artifacts lie scattered about.

The northerly and largest feature can be best characterized as a very low cobble alignment (cobbles loosely placed), rectangular in plan (Fig. 18b). The low (8") (20 cm) alignment forms a square-like cleared area bounded on the north by the main ditch, on the south by an alignment about 40 feet (12 m) long, on the west by an alignment 50 feet (15 m) long, and on the east by an alignment 55 feet (17 m) long. This latter segment is best defined and borders the main dump. Small cobbles one to two courses high compose the feature. Stove pipe remnants about the "wall" indicate a structure was placed near here at one time. The alignment may have defined a living or activity area.

Conical Pit

To the south of the alignment and main dump area about 58 feet (18 m) is a circular, cone-shaped depression 22 feet (7 m) in diameter and about six feet (2 m) deep with a gravel and dirt pile adjoining to the south. Several liquor bottle parts were found in the vicinity. This depression may represent a partially collapsed vertical air shaft for the drift mines located over 150 yards (137 m) to the south-southeast below but just above Dry Creek. The two partially collapsed adits or inclined shafts were not explored. Alternatively, and more likely as expressed by LaLande (1981:302), "Hydraulic miners customarily delineated the probable geographic extent of their operation by digging a series of prospect holes or test pits, and thereby evaluated the variable financial returns expected from an entire terrace."

Possible Assay or Retort Area

Westerly of the main rock alignment about 40 feet (12 m) is a small area of five or so bricks (covered with slag) and a small pile of slag or similar materials. This might represent a small assay or retort area of unknown age.

Wagon Road

Running in an east-west direction along the northerly edge of the complex is an old wagon road overgrown with manzanita and other vegetation (Fig. 18c). The road is about 10 feet (3 m) wide. It connects the reservoir and the present town of Igo to the northwest.

The 1875 General Land Office survey plat (Appendix 1) illustrates this same road from Igo to the approximate reservoir location. An examination of a 1971 black and white aerial photograph (1:12,000)(0403-FI 8-34-5), on file with the Bureau of Land Management in Redding, shows a network of roads and trails throughout the vicinity, many apparently emanating from the Igo-Piety Hill area including one road found during the field survey.

ARTIFACTS

CHINESE CERAMIC TABLEWARE

Soup Spoons

Four fragmented ceramic soup spoons were found in the main dump, two of which are illustrated in Figs. 2a and 3d. All specimens have an unglazed ring-foot. Table 1 provides a listing of all artifacts by provenience and Table 2 presents measurements for the Chinese vessels.

Three of the specimens are Four Seasons or Four Flowers spoons. No basal markings are present on these spoons. The bowls are elongate with projecting sides and ends (Fig. 3d). The Four Seasons' (winter-fall) flowers (cherry or prunus, water lily or lotus, tree peony, and chrysanthemum) are painted rather crudely in overglaze polychrome (greens, pink) on the bowl's interior with the flowering cherry "growing" up the handle.

The last specimen represents a Winter Green or Celadon spoon (Fig. 2a). The base of the bowl, which lacks the light bluish-green glaze of the remainder of the spoon, is white glazed with a cobalt blue hand painted potter's mark (cf. Olsen 1978:18) (Fig. 2a). Olsen (1978:30) notes such brush strokes depict bamboo leaves, small flowers, and abstract designs. Similar Winter Green examples can still be purchased in San Francisco's Chinatown.

Winter Green (Celadon) Small Cups

Three Winter Green (Celadon) fragmented small cups from the main dump are represented in the assemblage (Fig. 2b). The foot rings are unglazed. The descriptions of such cups by Olsen (1978:30) closely fit these examples. The cup is characterized by a thick green celadon glaze over the exterior of the vessel, except the base. The interior and base are a paler, light green glaze. Two of these specimens exhibit no markings on the base common on other examples and on the soup spoon of similar ware. The third fragmentary base exhibits a blue marking remnant.

Bamboo Bowls

Sherds and bases of six and possibly seven Bamboo pattern medium-sized bowls were found in the main dump (Figs. 2c-f). This pattern is also known as Three Circles and Dragonfly, Longevity, Swatow, or Blue Flower ware.

Based on rim arc, these vessels are about 15 cm in diameter, have slightly curving sides, and ovate flanged rims. Unglazed base rings are present. Olsen (1978:18) has presented a description of a ware which applies to these sherds. The bowls are characterized by a grayish-blue overall glaze of differing shades on porcellaneous stoneware with underglazed blue floral designs painted on the exterior. On these vessels two adjoining rings encircle the bottom interior of the vessels and, on three of the vessels, a bluish or grayish line follows the rim on top or on the interior side. Three

Table 1
Artifact Distribution at CA-Sha-1512

	North (Small) Dump	South (Large or Main) Dump	General Area
Chinese Ceramic Tableware			
Soup Spoon - Winter Green		1	
Soup Spoon - Four Flowers		3	
Small Cups - Winter Green		3	
Bamboo Bowls		7	
Four Flowers Serving Bowls	1	5	
Four Flowers Dishes (small)		2	
Chinese Ceramic Food Storage Vessels			
Large Brownware Storage Jar			1
Widemouthed Brownware Food Jars and Lids		4 (each)	
Brownware Jug		1	
Brownware Ng Ka Py Bottles		2	
Mottled Green glazed Jars		2	
Opium Pipe Bowls			
Gray Earthenware Circular Banded		2	
Orange Earthenware Octagonal Faceted		1	
Opium Can		1	
Euro-American Ceramics			
Vitrified White Earthenware Cups			2
Vitrified White Earthenware Dinner Plates		2	
Vitrified White Earthenware Soup Bowl		1	
Vitrified White Earthenware Vase			1
Yellowware Tea Pot		1	
Porcelain Door Knob			1
Bricks			5
Glass Artifacts			
Lamp Chimney		1	
Lantern Chimney		1	
Window Glass		+	
Liquor Bottles	1	11	2
Stoneware Bottle			1
Household Jars		1	1
Medium Jars		1	

	North Dump	South Dump	General Area[a]
Metal Artifacts			
Nails – Square Cut		248+	
Nails – Wire		6+	
Self-Shooter Apparatus			1
Metal Boxes			3
D-Shaped Lid	1		
Metal Lids (square)			3
Rectangular Tin Cans (small)		1	
Rectangular Tin Cans (large)		3	1
D-Rings		9	
Hole-in-cap Cans			2
Slip-lid Can			1
Paint or Lard Can			1
Modified Hole-in-cap Can			1
Lever Lid		1	
Square Pan		1	
Shallow Pan		1	
Cast Iron Pan		1	
Tart Pan (?)		1	
Mason Jar Lid		1	
Pipe Elbow			1
Riveted Water Pipe Section			1
Water Pipe Coupler			1
Tin Bucket	1		
Bucket Side-Modified			1
Coffee Pot		1	
Axe Head			1
Screwdriver Bits		3	
Pick Binding			1
Shovel Shank		1	
Wire Pieces		13	
Wire Pot Hangers		2	
Wire Handles		3	
Cutlery Handle		1	
Bands or Straps		7	14
Stove Pipe		1	
Copper Sheathing		1	
Ammunition			
Winchester New Rival No. 12 Shotgun Shell		1	
Footwear Parts			
Heel			1
Insole			1
Totals:	4	360+	49
Grand Total:	413+		

21

Table 2
Chinese Ceramic Vessels' Measurements*

Item	Length/Height	Width/Diameter	Thickness
Four Flowers spoon	11.0(overall)		
bowl	5.2	4.3	1.4
Four Flowers spoon	11.0(overall)		
bowl	5.2	4.4	1.2
Four Flowers spoon	?		
bowl	?	?	1.2
Winter Green spoon	10.8(overall)		
bowl	5.3	5.2	1.4
Winter Green small cup	3.6	7.1	2.5-5.2
Winter Green small cup	4.0	7.2	2.5-5.7
Winter Green small cup	3.85	7.35	2.5-5.7
Bamboo bowl	?	15.0	4.2-5.4+
base ring	0.9	6.3	
base ring	1.1	6.3	
Four Flowers serving bowl	6.0	18.7	2.3-4.2
Four Flowers serving bowl	7.0	18.7	2.3-4.2
ring foot	1.0		0.3-5.4
Four Flowers small dish (2)	2.3	8.4	
foot rings	0.6,0.7	4.2, 4.3	
Large storage jar	?	12.2(base)	0.7
Wide mouthed food jar	ca.12.5-13.0	12.2	0.4
Wide mouthed food jar		8.0(inside)	0.4
mouth sections (2)		8.8(outside)	
lids (2)	0.8, 0.9	9.2	0.4
lids (2)	0.7	7.1	0.2
"Soy Sauce" jug	?	12.4(base)	0.4
spout	?	0.75(orifice)	
Ng Ka Py bottle	?	8.0(base)	0.4
Ng Ka Py bottle	?	8.5(base)	0.4
Mottled green glazed jar	?	7.2(mouth)	0.3
Mottled green glazed jar	?	6.5(mouth)	0.2

*All measurements in centimeters

FIGURE 2

a.   Winter Green soup spoon (238-29) with basal mark.

b.   Winter Green small cup (238-28).

c.   Rim sherd of Bamboo pattern bowl (238-37).

d.   Base of Bamboo pattern bowl (238-65) with
        mark on interior bottom.

e.   Rim sherd of Bamboo pattern bowl (238-35).

f.   Rim sherd of Bamboo pattern bowl (238-36).

FIGURE 2

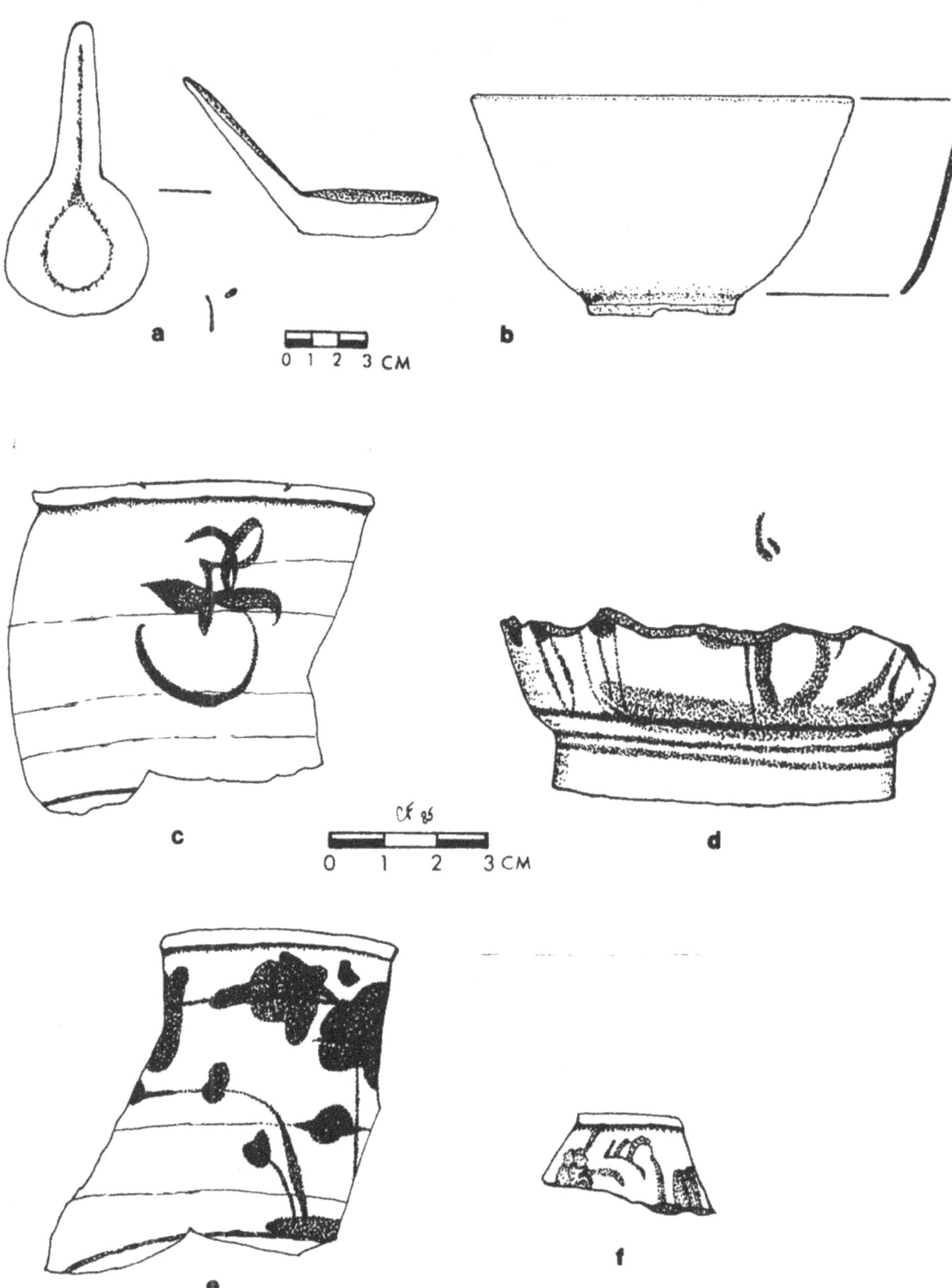

a

0 1 2 3 CM

b

c

CF 85

0 1 2 3 CM

d

e

f

FIGURE 3

a. Four Flowers pattern serving bowl (238-25a) with floral medallion and basal seal.

b. Four Flowers pattern serving bowl (238-25b) with floral medallion.

c. Basal sherd of Four Flowers pattern serving bowl (238-47) illustrating seal and floral medallion.

d. Four Flowers pattern soup spoon (238-27).

FIGURE 3

a

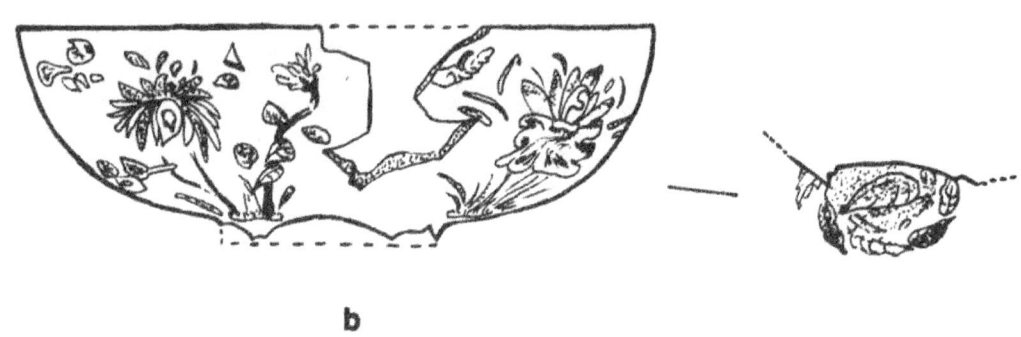

b

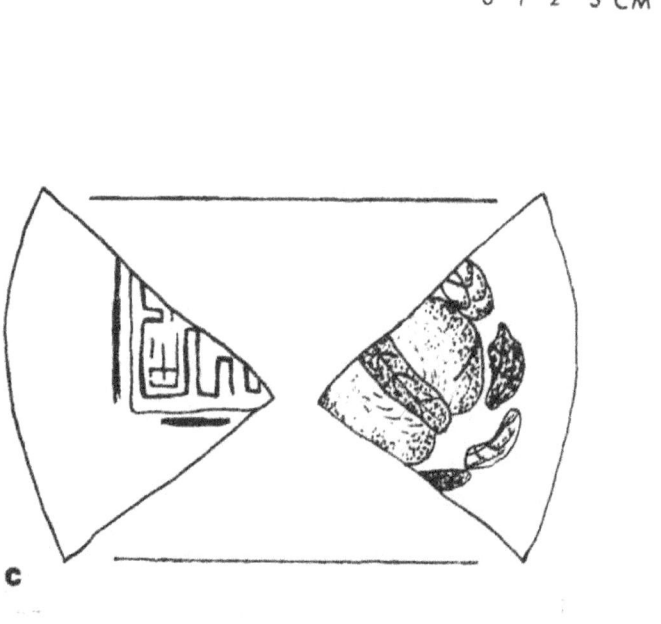

c

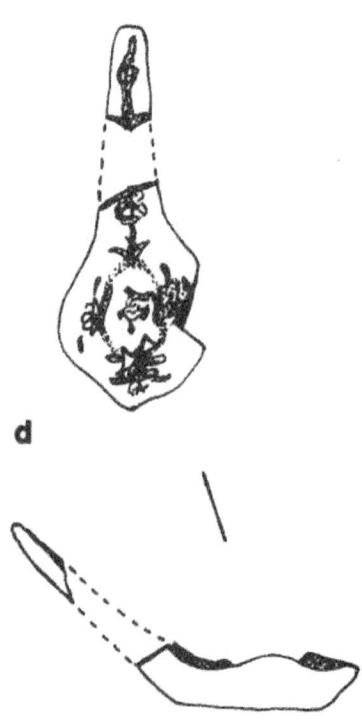

d

0 1 2 3 CM

26

blue lines also encircle the exterior base, two on the foot ring and one exterior near the base.

As noted by Felton et al. (1984:41), Chace (1976:523), Olsen (1978:15-16), and Praetzellis and Praetzellis (1979:149-150), the pattern, relative number and identity of the decoration elements are consistent whereas the quality of treatment (as evidenced on these sherds) varies with many decorations not carefully executed. One vessel exhibits interior and exterior pattern marks. On the base is a faint orangish seal. The interior mark is blue with adjoining short, straight and comma-like brush lines (Fig. 2d).

Felton et al. (1984:41) note that bowls of this type are common on North American sites with Chinese use. This type of ware has a long history with little stylistic change over time (cf. Olsen 1978:16).

Four Flowers Vessels

The Four Flowers (also designated Four Seasons or Enameled Flowerware) pattern is represented at this site by eight porcelain vessels; five serving bowls, two small dishes, and one probable serving bowl (Figs. 2a-c). A short bowl is from the north dump while the other bowls are from the nearby larger south dump.

The two small dishes are about one-half present. One dish closely matches Chace's (1976:525) measurements for this vessel form (Table 2).

The decoration of these bowls and dishes consists of a thick overglazed enameled floral design of greens, pink, brown, and orange on a white background. Aside from the four floral designs mentioned in the spoon discussion, there is a round, floral medallion on the interior bottom of these vessels (Figs. 3a-c). The designs on the dishes and spoons are inferior to those on the bowls.

One of the bowls and the two small dishes contain orange or orangish-red pattern marks or square seals which are too faint or poorly executed to be translated (Fig. 3a). These marks are 1.3 cm square on the dishes and 2 cm square on the bowl. In addition, a basal sherd of a bowl exhibits an orangish base mark or reign mark (Fig. 3c) which might be a Kuang Xu seal dated from 1875-1909 (Priscilla Wegars, University of Idaho, Personal Communication 1985; Andacht et al. 1984:264).

CHINESE CERAMIC FOOD STORAGE VESSELS

Fragments of at least eight vessels of brown glazed stoneware were recovered, seven from the main dump area. Also recovered were parts of two mottled green glazed jars and another mottled glazed vessel of unknown shape but probably in the same class. These vessels served mainly in the storage and marketing of various food products ranging from liquor to dried fish and vegetables. Such forms are ubiquitous within 19th century overseas Chinese sites (Felton et al. 1984:42) and are not time-sensitive. Forms include jars, jugs, bottles, and lids. Ferraro and Ferraro (1965) label these vessels "min gei" meaning folk art or people's art.

The cream- to buff-colored paste stoneware vessels are coated (except on lids and the exterior bases of the jars and jugs) with a thick, shiny brown to dark brown ash glaze. This glaze seems especially coarse on brownware jugs. Olsen (1976:36) notes this glaze is a descendant of an original Sung dynasty glaze. Ferraro and Ferraro (1965:28) indicate that these vessels have been formed by pressing clay into top and bottom molds, the two halves being joined by a slip and (in several of these examples) with a band of clay evident on the vessel's interior. The flanged lip was later added, at least on the "whiskey" and jug vessels. Because of a lack of standardization the vessels vary somewhat in shape.

Large Storage Jar

The slightly concave partial base of a large storage jar or urn was recovered from the surface of the site near the dumps. The exact configuration of the vessel is uncertain but the base diameter and acutely sloping, thick sidewall suggest a large jar, perhaps similar to the vessel illustrated in Ferraro and Ferraro (1965:20), Brott (1982:Fig. 24), and Felton et al. (1984:Fig. 10d).

Widemouthed Food Jars and Lids

Based on rim and base reconstructions there are at least three widemouthed, shouldered, brown-glazed storage or food jars. Recovered lid fragments indicate at least four such vessels are present, two of the smaller (around 1 lb.) size and two of the larger (around 2 lbs.) size (Figs. 4b, 4g) (Felton et al. 1984:Fig. 11c).

The recovered lids represent slightly concave discs with tapered rims which are slightly larger than the jar orifices. According to Felton et al. (1984:47), they were apparently placed on the jar top, concave face up and sealed with clay (Figs. 4e, 4f). A long list of products stored in these jars, including vegetables, sauces or pastes, pickled or salted items, sea food, tea, oils, and other liquids, is provided by Felton et al. (1984:47).

Brownware Jug

One brownware "soy sauce" jug was recovered based on the presence of a spout (Fig. 4d) and matching sherds. These vessels are virtually the same as the food storage vessels described above except for the spout and mouth (see Felton et al. 1984:47). Examples of this vessel are illustrated by Ferraro and Ferraro (1965:21), Chace (1976:516), Brott (1982:Fig. 23), and Felton et al. (1984:Fig. 11b). Olsen (1978:36) notes that aside from soy sauce, such pots were also used to transport and store fine black vinegar and thick molasses, the latter an important sweet to the Chinese.

Brownware Ng Ka Py Bottles

Two brownware Ng Ka Py liquor bottles (sometimes labeled wine bottles) were identified by the presence of two brown-glazed stoneware bases (Fig. 4c). These vessels are globular or tear-drop

FIGURE 4

a. Rim section of mottled green glazed stoneware "ginger" jar (238-46).

b. Rim section of widemouthed, shouldered, brown-glazed stoneware storage or food jar (238-13a).

c. Interior basal section of brown-glazed stoneware Ng Ka Py bottle (238-13b).

d. Spout from brown-glazed stoneware "soy sauce" jug (238-10) (see Figure 4g).

e. Unglazed stoneware lid from storage or food jar (238-6).

f. Unglazed stoneware lid from storage or food jar (238-5).

g. Bottom portion of brown-glazed stoneware storage or food jar (238-15).

FIGURE 4

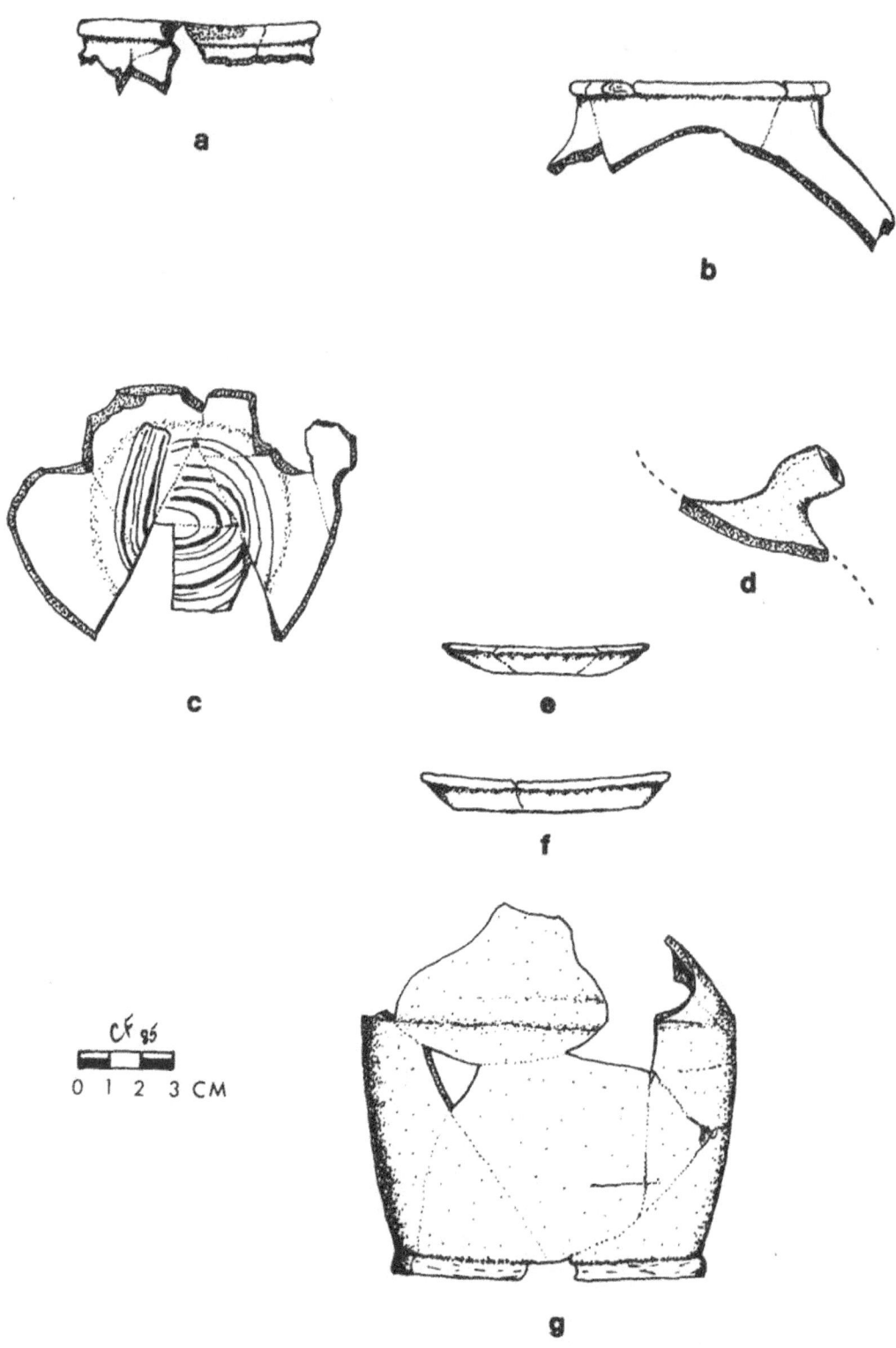

a

b

c

d

e

f

CF 85

0 1 2 3 CM

g

shaped with a flaring neck and mouth (cf. Ferraro and Ferraro 1965:20; Chace 1976:515; Brott 1982:Fig. 23; and Felton et al. 1984:Fig. 11a). The bases on the two specimens in this sample are 8.0 and 8.5 cm. The foot rings are not glazed and are flattish in shape.

Ferraro and Ferraro (1965:28) note that these bottles often contained Ng Ka Py, a 96 proof whiskey sometimes called tiger whiskey or "wine", a generic designation for liquor in Chinese (cf. Chace 1976:517, and Olsen 1976:36).

Such bottles are still offered for sale at San Francisco Chinatown's liquor stores, although the modern brown glaze is often much lighter.

Mottled Green Glazed Jars

The remains of two shattered, mottled green glazed jars were recovered from the main dump area (Fig. 4a). The glaze on the first is iridescent with blue and black colors of minor content. The second jar is mottled green. The stoneware jars are composed of a light, yellowish-brown stoneware clay with no apparent glazing on the interior except on the expanding, slightly convex topped rim. It would appear these jars were constructed in two halves in a wheel centered exterior mold and later seamed together. Several fragments exhibit only partial glazing on the exterior and back wall, indicating the bases were not glazed and an apparent poor overall firing or glazing of the vessel.

These specimens match closely the ginger jar described by Chace (1976:522) from Ventura and less closely those described and illustrated by Olsen (1978:34-35) from Tucson, Arizona. A nearly identical example from Weaverville is on display at the Trinity County Museum. Olsen (1978:35) notes such jars were used to hold a variety of products other than ginger such as preserved chopped garlic, sliced turnips, fish, green onions, sweet gerkins, and green plums.

A mid-body sherd of a thicker (0.25 cm) jar glazed in mottled blue-black and honey colors on the exterior and honey colored on the interior was found in the main dump. It matches no other sherd found (compare Teague and Shenk 1977:106). The interior of the sherd exhibits a clay band indicative of two-piece mold construction. This may be a fragment of a storage vessel, perhaps similar to the jars illustrated by Ferraro and Ferraro (1965:28) or one of the older ware bottle types discussed by Olsen (1978:49).

OPIUM PIPE BOWLS

During the course of artifact recovery, fragments of three earthenware Chinese opium pipe bowls were recovered from the south dump. Two of these specimens are gray stoneware pipe bowls (Fig. 5b). One specimen is nearly complete. This specimen is 5.9 cm in diameter and approximately 3.5 cm in height. The bowl falls within the circular, banded type of Felton et al. (1984:65), although it differs slightly from the type illustrated. The side of the bowl is

FIGURE 5

a. Opium pipe bowl section manufactured from orangish stoneware with orange glaze. Bowl is of the hexagonal faceted type (238-52).

b. Gray stoneware opium bowl of the circular banded type (238-30). Money mark and other symbols illustrated from base.

c. Vitrified white earthenware cup or small bowl (238-39).

d. Vitrified white earthenware cup or small bowl (238-40).

e. Vitrified white earthenware dinner plate portion with partial basal hallmark illustrated (238-41).

FIGURE 5

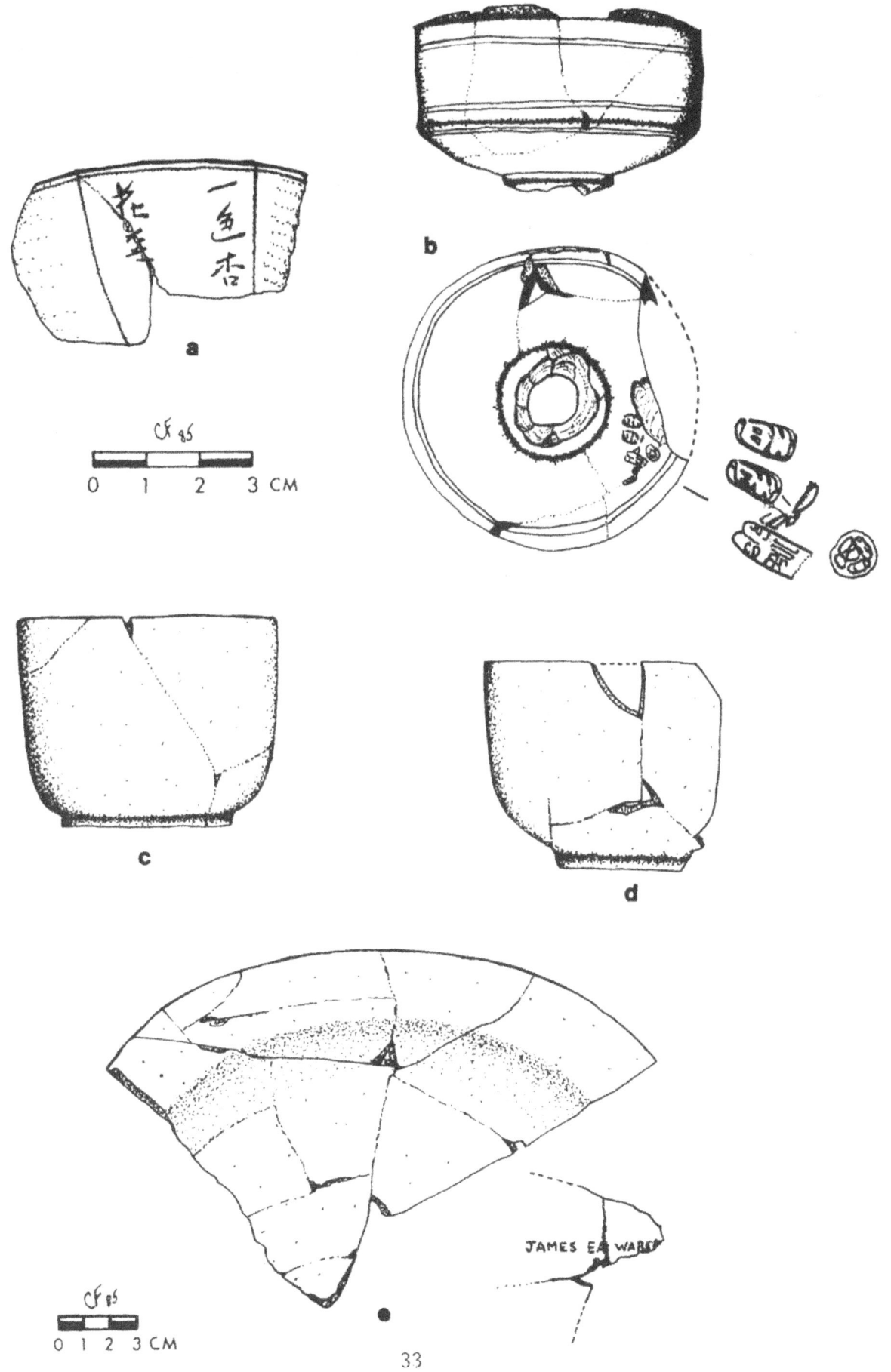

33

minimally concave and there is an incised, double-lined band near the upper and lower portion of the side and on the base near the outer edge. The base of the bowl contains a money mark and other symbols, some faint, that appear to indicate Prosperity Store and Ji'Ji' or Double Lucky, common to opium pipe bowls (cf. Wegars 1981:6) (Fig. 5b) (Appendix 2).

A second opium bowl fragment is also gray stoneware of the circular type but without apparent decoration. The sides appear more concave than the first specimen. A number of these type are exhibited at the Joss House in Weaverville.

The third bowl fragment is of the hexagonal faceted type of Felton et al. (1984:65), manufactured from an orangish stoneware with polished exterior (Fig. 5a). The fragment bears Chinese characters on the bowl face that express a common spontaneous Chinese saying describing the apricot flower in blossom (Priscilla Wegars, personal communication 1985) (Appendix 2).

OPIUM CAN

A partial lid and side of a brass opium can were uncovered in the main deposit area. The lid is 4 cm wide and about 6.5 cm in length composed of 0.3 cm thick metal. A stamped mark on the lid corresponds with the "Li Yun" or "Beautiful Origin" brand of opium as illustrated in Felton et al. (1984:Fig. 166). In addition there is a partial black-painted Chinese character of unknown meaning.

EURO-AMERICAN CERAMICS

Vitrified White Earthenware (Ironstone)

Two hollow-ware vessels and five flatware vessels were recovered from the site; the latter five (one complete, the others fragmentary) are from the main dump area and the former two are from the surface south of this dump. Measurements are provided in Table 3.

The two undecorated cups or small bowls (Figs. 5c, 5d), designated St. Denis bowls in the Butler Brothers Catalogue (1915), have glazed foot-rings and tapering rims. Maker's marks are not present possibly due to the fragmentary nature of the bases.

The undecorated flatware vessels include two dinner plates, one soup plate, a probable saucer and one small vessel. All have foot rings and maker's marks or portions thereof.

One plate is impressed JAMES EDWARDS with a printer's hallmark of the Victorian Royal Arms (seated) above STONE CHINA above JAMES EDWARDS & SON above DALEHALL. This is Figure 103 in Praetzellis et al. (1983) dated 1852-1882 (Fig. 5e). This pottery was made in Burslem, Staffordshire, England. The second plate, a basal section, has remnants of the ceramic mark identified as that of Knowles, Taylor and Knowles Co. of East Liverpool, Ohio (Gates and Ormerod 1982:Fig. 99a) circa 1885 to 1907. The trademark includes an eagle within a badge over which is printed IRON STONE CHINA and under which is printed KNOWLES, TAYLOR AND KNOWLES.

TABLE 3

Euro-American Ceramics' Measurements*

Artifact	Diameter/Length	Height	Thickness
Vitrified white earthenware			
cup or small bowl (2)	4-1/2	3-1/2	
dinner plate (2)	9-1/2	1	
soup plate	9-1/2	2	
saucer (2)	?	?	
vase	4 (base)	?	
Common pottery (Yellowware)			
teapot	4-1/4 (base)	?	
	3/4 (spout)	?	
Stoneware bottle	2-15/16	?	
Porcelain doorknob	2		
Bricks	7+	5	2-1/2

*All measurements in inches

The saucer has a very fragmentary ceramic mark including the hind end of the lion on the Victorian Royal Arms (standing). A close comparison with those illustrated by Praetzellis et al. (1983:Fig. 129; 40-41) suggests it may be of W. H. Grindley & Co. of Tunstall, Staffordshire, England dating from 1891-1925.

In addition, fragments of a small, thin vessel, also possibly a saucer, were recovered.

Along the bulldozed road adjoining the main dump occur sherds of a probable vase, polygonal in outline (octagonal?). The lip is scalloped and bands run across the vessel near the top and bottom.

The soup plate has the printed Victorian Royal Arms (seated) above "WARRANTED STONE CHINA" above "R. COCHRAN & Co. GLASGOW". This earthenware, according to Praetzellis et al. (1983:24 Fig. 746), dates from 1846-1918 (Fig. 6).

Common Pottery (Yellowware)

A molded teapot earthenware base, body parts, and spout, were recovered in the main dump area (Fig. 7). The spout exhibits a ribbed or banded appearance as illustrated. The body includes various bands and wide ribs.

The specimen has a buff to light yellow fabric with a clear, lead glaze providing a light yellow color to the exterior and interior surfaces. Hamilton and Hall (1982:ware type 27) note that this type of ceramic was manufactured in Great Britain, North America, Europe and Asia from 1850 to present, but with a peak of popularity from 1870 to 1900. According to Priscilla Wegars (personal communication 1985) this is probably of Euro-American manufacture.

Stoneware Bottle

A cream-colored salt-glazed stoneware ale bottle base was found along a feeder ditch about halfway between Igo and the subject reservoir. Along the side at the base is an oval impression with GLASGOW in the center, PORT-DUNDAS over the top and POTTERY Coy beneath. Two small crosses occur along each side. According to Fleming (1923:226-227) and Godden (1972:186-187), this pottery remained in existence from 1845 to 1932. However, "Ltd" was added to the firm's style in 1905.

Porcelain Doorknob

A fragmented white glaze porcelain doorknob was noted along the bulldozed road by the main dump, perhaps a component of the dump disturbed by this road.

BRICKS

In the small "assay" area just west of the dumps and along the main ditch were found four of five rectangular, fired, buff-colored bricks of coarse-textured fabric. All of the bricks are broken. Two of the

FIGURE 6

Vitrified white earthenware soup plate and basal hallmark (238-43).

FIGURE 6

WARRANTED STONE CHINA
FL COCHRAN & C⁰ GLASGOW

0 1 2 3 CM

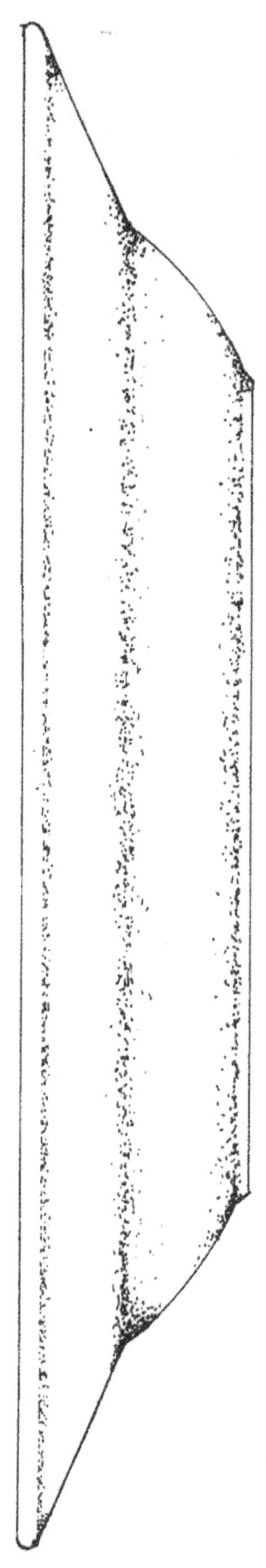

FIGURE 7

Sections of yellow earthenware molded teapot (238-75).

FIGURE 7

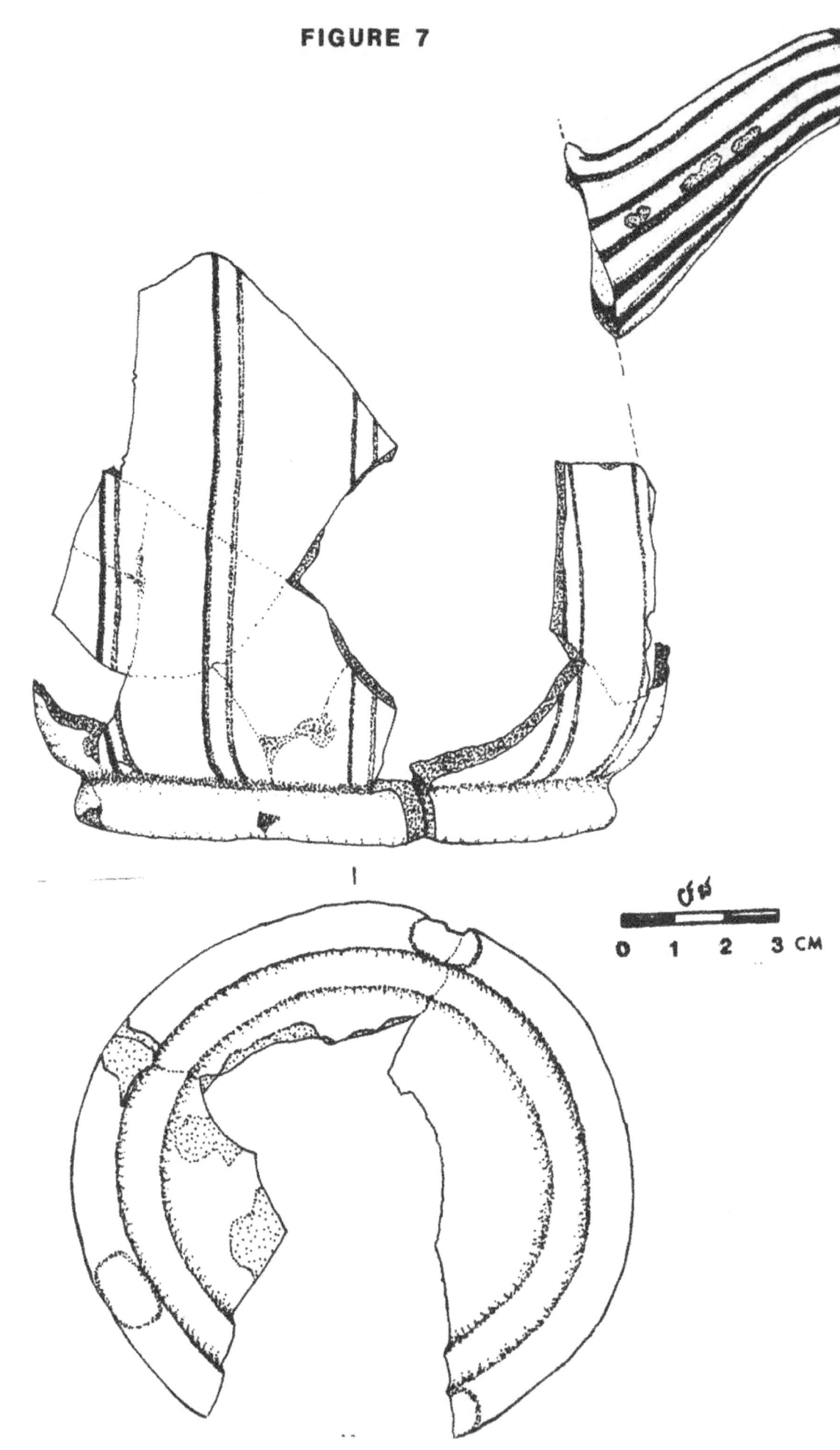

bricks have stamped letters, apparently maker's marks. Only portions of the trade names are visible--one is MP or MR and another has the letter N on it. Most of the brick fragments are covered on one side with a slag-like material. It is possible this feature area post-dates the Chinese use owing to several Depression-era artifacts nearby (within 15 m or so).

GLASS ARTIFACTS

Lamp and Lantern Chimneys

Fragments of a thin (1/16") lamp and two thick (1/8") lantern chimneys were found in the main dump. About one half of the lamp fragments are clear glass while the remainder exhibit purple or amethyst coloring indicative of manganese addition to the glass most common between 1880 and 1914 (Kendrick 1964:43). Several of the pieces are bordered by a scalloped edge prevalent on lamp chimneys (see Berge 1980:154). According to Lorrain (1968:44), kerosene lamps began to appear in the 1860s.

Also found were the purple glass fragments of two lantern chimney bases and crowns, both with rim grinding. One fragment (of the crown) exhibits the end of a word ...tz, probably a Dietz lantern chimney ca. 1902 (see Amory 1969). The lantern chimney pieces match those exhibited by Berge (1980:Fig. 69b, d). The base of these two chimneys, each with a flaring ring (one rounded, the other downward tapering) are four inches in diameter.

Window Glass

Nine fragments of window pane glass were found in the main dump area nearest the bulldozed road (more would have been found in this area with screening).

The average thickness of the window glass is 0.085" (based on the mean of five readings). If Chance and Chance's (1976:252) suggested age ranges from historic Vancouver, Washington can be applied then a date of 1855 to 1885 for manufacture-use can be ascribed to the glass.

Glass Liquor Bottles

The remains of at least 14 and possibly 15 glass liquor bottles were recovered from the site complex, and fragments (green colored) of other possible bottles were noted. These recovered bottle remains are listed below.

Green finish, neck and shoulder. Champagne finish with slightly tapering neck (Fig. 8a). Swirl patterns evident on neck as found on fancy liquor bottles (Berge 1980:58). No seam present (main dump).

Green neck and finish (Fig. 8b). Brandy finish, no seams evident; tapered neck (main dump).

Green/yellow neck and finish. Brandy finish with swirl-pattern tapered neck (Fig. 8c) (main dump).

FIGURE 8

a. Olive-green champagne or wine bottle shoulder, neck and finish (champagne) (238-87a).

b. Green liquor bottle neck and finish (brandy) (238-87b).

c. Green-yellow liquor bottle neck and finish (brandy) with swirl pattern (238-87c).

d. Green liquor bottle neck and finish (brandy) (238-87d).

FIGURE 8

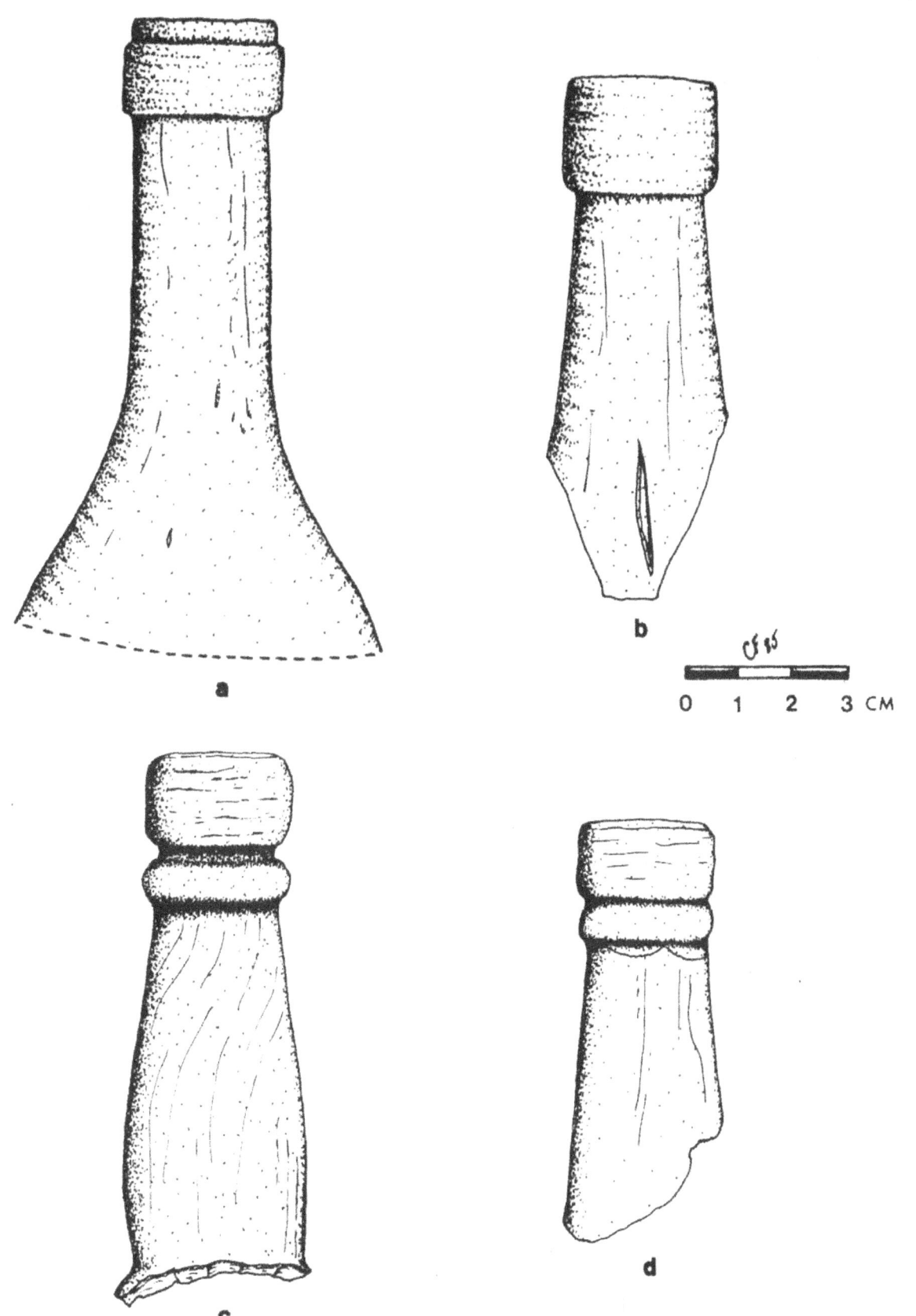

a

b

c

d

0 1 2 3 CM

Olive-green neck and finish. Champagne finish, no seam evident; tapered neck (dump area).

Green neck and shoulder. Bulbous neck possibly with swirl pattern. Body about 3-1/8" diameter. Mold produced, seams not evident on shoulder (secondary dump). Horizontal striation from turn mold. According to Kendrick (1964:31), these molds were invented about 1860 and became most common between 1880 and 1900.

Green neck and finish. Brandy finish with cork still present. Bulbous neck possibly exhibiting swirl patterns. No seams evident (main dump).

Green finish. Brandy finish with probable tapering neck (main dump) (Fig. 8d).

Green neck and finish. Oil (ring) finish. Swirl pattern evident on tapering neck. No seams present on neck (main dump).

Amber base (2) with one inch deep molded kick up. Produced from a turn mold. Base 3 1/8" diameter (main dump).

Amber base fragment, possibly similar to the previous two examples with kick ups (main dump).

Amber base kick-up portion. Probably similar to other bases described above but slightly shallower (main dump).

Amber neck and finish. Brandy finish, no seams evident; tapered neck. Possible swirl patterns on neck. Probably matches one of bases described above (main dump).

Amber base and body fragments. Seams evident from mold production. Flat base with no marks evident (3 1/8" diameter). Use of a snap in bottle production eliminated pontil marks and was used through the 1880s (Kendrick 1969:20-21) (main dump).

Light green base fragments. Circular with remnants of embossed star. Side seam partially across slightly recessed base and ring seam around base. This may be from a post-bottom mold but more likely from an automatic bottle machine. Jones notes (1971:8) automatic bottle machines began in 1903. The star may be a trade mark of the Southern Glass Company of Los Angeles dating from 1919 to 1929 (Jones 1966:18), but earlier manufacture by other companies is also possible (cf. Toulouse 1971:486-487).

With the exception of the last example, these bottles all seem to approximate the 4/5th quart or 1 liter size (or thereabouts) and held such liquor as wine and whiskey. Chance and Chance (1976:139) note that amber or brown glass bottles began gaining popularity over the dark olive-green bottle (at the Kanaka Village/Vancouver Barracks, anyhow) after 1876. All recovered liquor bottles are of the molded variety lacking pontil marks with applied lips dating from about 1860 to 1900 (Kendrick 1964:21, 33).

Household Jars

A shattered light green Mason jar was recovered from the main dump area. A similar example is illustrated and described in Berge (1980:Fig. 47, pgs. 100-102).

The recovered specimen is embossed on the body with MASON'S/PATENT/ NOV. 30TH/1858. A Maltese cross is also present on the body. The closure was screw top, fragments of which were recovered and are described elsewhere. The finish is threaded seal with a ground top. The jar's body is cylindrical with a flat shoulder. The opening of the jar is 2-1/2" with a base 4" in diameter. The base is embossed with PAT/NOV/26/67 around the circumference with mold set numbers 89 or 68 in the center. Height exceeded 6" suggesting this was a two-quart size jar.

According to Berge (1980:100), the date this bottle was in use runs from 1860 until 1913. Other companies used the same inscription on their jars. Berge (1980:52) notes that the Hero Fruit Jar Company marked their jars with a Maltese cross and HERO. Perhaps this is one of their jars.

Kendrick (1964:37) states that the earlier jars can be separated from later ones by the ground rims, apparently prior to 1892. Jones (1971:10) indicates the practice became obsolete by 1915.

Seams run the entire side of the jar, from rim onto base and a circular seam is present around the base probably as a result of the post-bottom mold process (see Berge 1980:64).

A second purple-tinted food jar top was found on the surface in the vicinity of the main dump (Fig. 12a). The diameter of the base is two inches, suggesting this was about a quart in capacity. The top is a broad glass ring like the packer finish (sealing surface) but with an indented ring around the top of the finish (cf. Berg 1980:Fig. 58). This jar was probably produced in a dip or turn mold. The coloring of this jar, indicative of a manganese addition to the glass, suggests an 1880 to circa 1914 date (Kendrick 1964:43).

Purple glass fragments from what appears to be a medium-sized jar with threaded closure were found in the main dump area. The function of this jar is unknown.

In general, the glass artifacts from the site suggest primary deposition (site use) during the 1880s to 1890s.

METAL ARTIFACTS

Nails

Both wire and common cut ferrous nails were recovered from the main dump during screening. By far, common cut were the most frequent with 248 nails, 167 of which were 7d. Only six wire nails were recovered. The size breakdown is presented in Table 4. Some may be burnt but rusting makes such identification difficult.

Table 4
Nails by Penny Weight

	Unk.	4d	5d	6d	7d	8d	9d	12d	16d	Total
Wire		1	1	1		3				6
Common Cut	20				167	27	3	26	5	248
Total	20	1	1	1	167	30	3	26	5	254

These numbers do not include all nails in the main dump, merely a grab sample of perhaps 1/2 of those present (all recovered in the screen).

A little over 80% of the nails are straight, the rest exhibiting obvious bending up to 90° indicating probable utilization (and forced removal) in a wooden structure. The size range is consistent with lumber-frame buildings or other structures (cf. LaLande 1981:110).

Cut nails generally pre-date the 1890s (Fontana 1965:89), and the few wire nails probably represent the tail end of site use (or structure construction/repair) near the beginning of the 20th century.

Square cut nails were also observed on the ground around the small rock feature just south of the main deposition area. They appeared to be within the same size range and frequency as were the square cut nails (and one wire nail) observed in the main deposition area not screened. Additionally, several medium-sized square cut nails were noted along the berm of the reservoir.

Self-Shooter Apparatus or Gate Mechanism

On the south abutment of the reservoir outlet chute was recovered a hand-made problematic ferrous metal apparatus (Fig. 9a). Various parts of other artifacts have been integrated to form this piece of machinery.

The specimen includes a 13" long metal pin 5/8 " thick with a truss head on one end and an eyelet on the other. Through the eyelet is a 1/2" thick rectangular link (8" x 3 1/2") which is in turn attached to a double twisted and partially folded metal strip or band 1" wide and 1/4" thick. The attachment is at the fold. One end of the band has been cut and a hook 1" wide is present on the other end. Wire 1/16" thick is wrapped around the hook and around the two arms of the metal band. Two holes 1/8" in diameter have been drilled through the metal, perhaps at one time prior to its re-use to attach the band to a board.

It seems evident the two ends of the apparatus were attached to other features. The location of the item, associated with two granite blocks and a wood beam at the reservoir outlet, suggests use in a self-shooter with the hook attached to the gate portion and then pinned to a foundation of some sort. Self-shooters were contrivances for collecting and discharging water as in booming or ground sluicing for gold, evidence of which is found below the reservoir chute.

FIGURE 9

a. Self-shooter or gate apparatus from reservoir outlet (238-94).

b. Hand-fabricated metal and wood box with side and base
    illustrated (238-90).

FIGURE 9

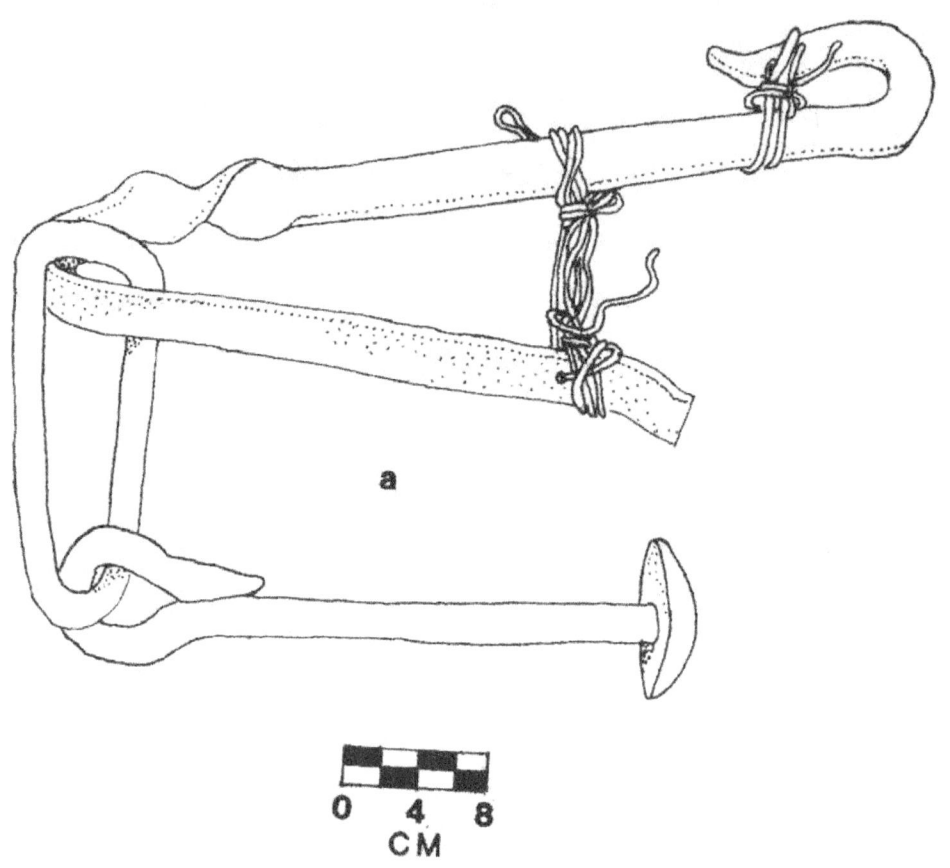

a

0 4 8
CM

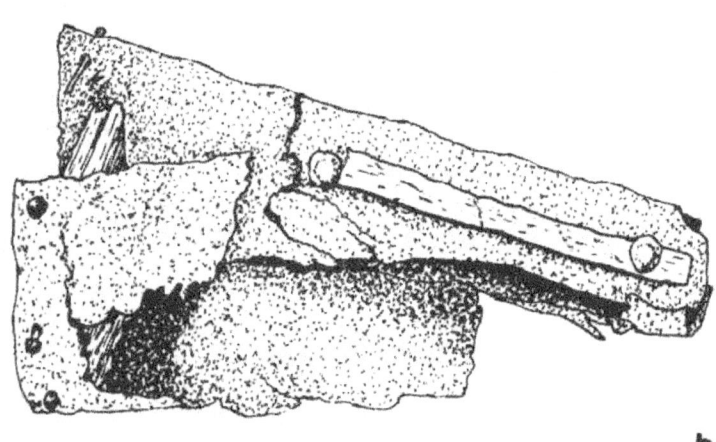

b

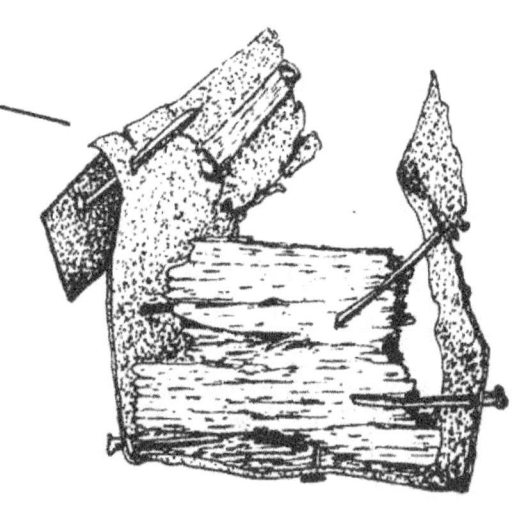

0 1 2 3 CM

Cans, Pans, and Containers

Between the dump and reservoir was recovered a handmade metal box
(Fig. 9b). The partially deteriorated box has a thick wooden base
attached to the metal sheet sidings by seven or more 4d common cut
nails. Along one side of the box, metal bands have been attached by
galvanized rivets. Measurements for artifacts in this section are
presented in Table 5. This box was sturdy, apparently utilized for
heavy-duty storage.

Two additional all-metal boxes were found between the main dump and
the reservoir. The first box at one time included a lid hinged on
the side, subsequently snapped off. The second box is solder
seamed. The top has been cut one-half way down each side forming a
flap.

Three heavy-duty, hand-fabricated metal lids were found on the
surface of the site. All are of thick metal. The first lid has two
1/4" holes punched 1/2" and 2" from the edge, centrally placed and
the second lid has holes 1/4" in diameter drilled along one edge with
remnants of a riveted strap on the top.

A rectangular lid to a fish or meat can was recovered in the main
dump (Fig. 12c). The impression of a key 3-1/2" long is present. A
3" wide section of another can probably of similar age and function
was found near the dump. Rock (1984:100) has noted that key-wind
opened cans were begun to be manufactured by 1866, but they weren't
practical until the 1890's.

Also recovered in the same dump were the badly decomposing pieces of
large, rectangular iron cans with hand-soldered lap side seams. A
tin spout suggests one of the vessels may have been a syrup, honey or
oil container (Fig. 10b). Another fragment of the container has a
looped wire handle still attached to a D-ring. An added twisted wire
handle and D-ring were probably attached to a can as well. These
cans may have been used to carry water or other liquids. Hand
soldered tins like these were common until the 1880s (Rock 1984:103).

Four side or end pieces of a tin container, probably of those
described above, exhibit patched circular holes (Fig. 10a). Jim Rock
of the Klamath National Forest in Yreka, California (personal
communication 1985) notes that this form of sealing dates from at
least the 1860s and later. Priscilla Wegars (personal communication
1985) suggests these tins may have originated in China, used in
importing oil and other substances. Judith Tordoff (personal
communication 1986) indicates quite a few of these were found during
the nearby Cottonwood project work.

Besides the D-rings described above, seven others were found in the
main dump. Six of the seven are attached to tin can remnants
suggesting (in conjunction with the other D-ring remnants) at least
five canisters of at least three different sizes are present (Fig.
10d).

In the vicinity of the main dump lying about on the surface were a
number of tin cans of various sizes and functions discussed below.

49

TABLE 5

Cans, Pans and Containers' Measurements (in inches)

Artifact	Length/Height	Diameter/Width	Thickness/Depth
Handmade metal box	8-1/2	3-1/2	1/2 (wooden base)
attached band	8	1-1/2	1/16
attached band	5-3/4	1/2 (galv)	1/16
Metal box	6	4	2
Metal box	7-1/4	3	2
Metal lid	9	7	1 (1/16 th)
Metal lid	10	8	1-1/2 (1/16 th)
Metal lid	9	1/2	3/4 (1/16 th)
Fish/meat tin lid	4	3	?
Large rectangular tin	?	4	2
Large rectangular tin	10	?	2
D-ring	1-1/2	3/4	1/16
D-ring	2-1/2	1	1/16
D-ring (4)	1-1/4	3/4	1/16
D-ring (2)	1-5/8	5/8	1/16
D-ring	7/8	5/8	1/16
Tin spout	3/4	1-1/2 - 1-1/4	?
Tin container patch (2)	1-3/4 (hole)	2 (square)	1/32
Tin container	6-1/2	6-1/2	?
Tin container	8	5-1/2	?
Hole-in-cap can	4-3/8	3-1/2	
Hole-in-cap can	6	4	
Hole-in-cap can	4-3/16	?	
Slip lid top can	5-1/2	4	
Slip lid	?	?	
Paint or lard can	6	3-1/2	
D-shaped lid	15-1/2	6-5/8	
Tin lever-lid	1/4	11-1/4	
Handle	8	7-1/2	3/16
Shallow pan		12	
Cast iron pan	1-1/4 ht.		1/4 (footring)
"Tart" pan		5	
fluted edge		1	
Mason jar cap		3	
Pipe elbow	11	5-1/2	
metal bands			1/8
Tin bucket	12	9	
Modified bucket	13	9	
attached band	5	1-3/4	1/8
attached band	4	1-3/4	1/8
Coffee pot	9	8	

FIGURE 10

a.   Portion of large rectangular storage tin (oil?) exhibiting square patch over hole (238-108).

b.   Tin spout from large can (238-102).

c.   Fragment of possible cooking pan of cast iron (238-46).

d.   D-ring attached to edge of large rectangular tin can (238-107).

FIGURE 10

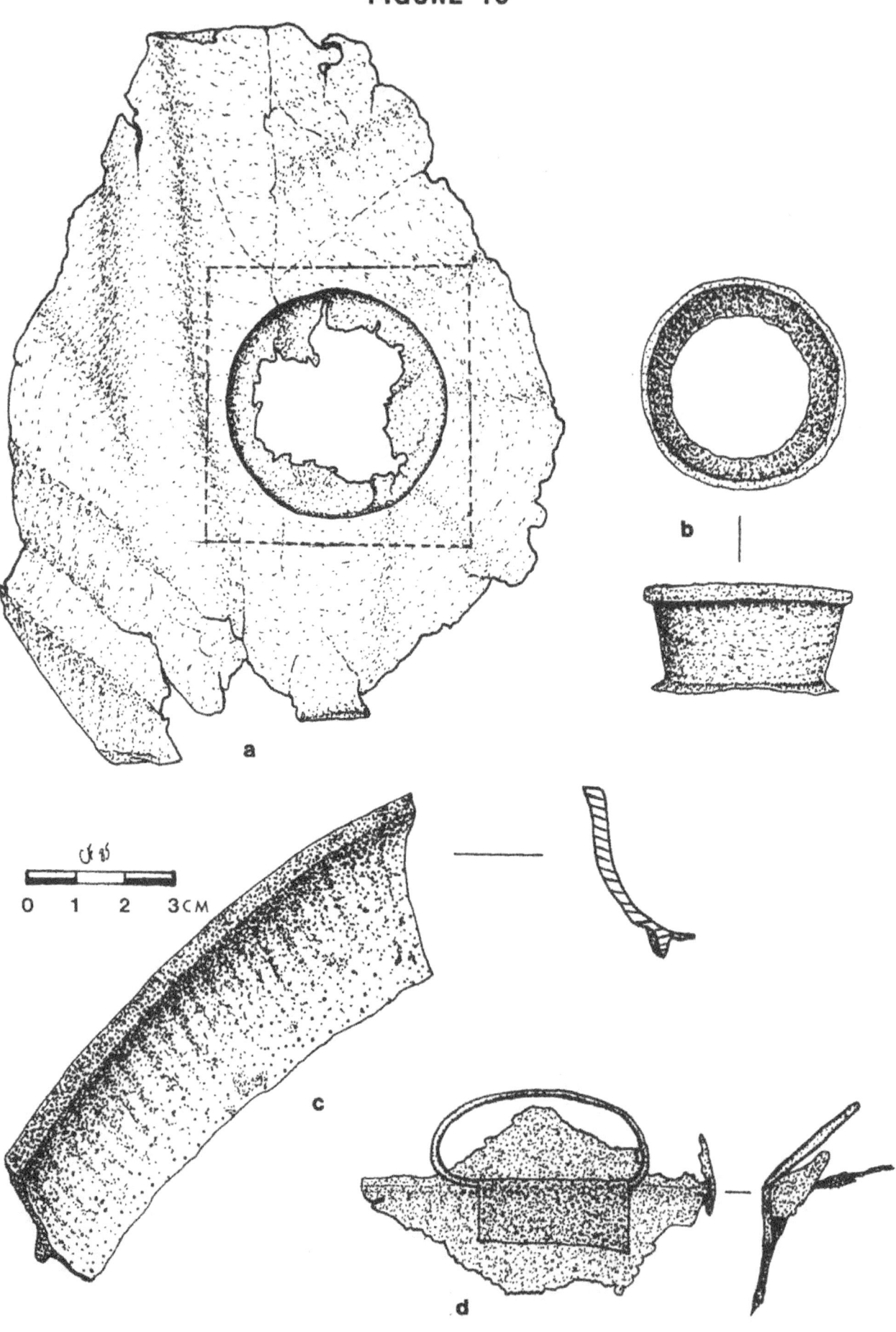

0 1 2 3CM

Two probable hole-in-cap food cans were found.   One is a No.   2-1/2 can.

A can with a slip-lid top was found with a later-added wire handle. A similar example is illustrated in Clark (1977:65)   and   Keen (1982:Fig.   17).   Such cans initially held dry goods such as pepper or carbide.

A misshapen paint or lard can was recovered from the site.

A portion of a modified tin can, possibly a hole-in-cap can, was recovered.   This artifact has a wire handle attached between the ends and exhibits five large-size square-cut nail holes punched in a domino pattern on the side.   What function this object held, other than serving or sprinkling, is unknown.

At the small northerly dump, on the surface, occurred a sheet metal lid, D-shaped with hinges and a wire-reinforced edge.

A tin lever-lid similar to that illustrated in Keen (1982:metal container) and Woolfenden (1970:228) may be a lid to a pan or lard bucket (Fig. 11).   A D-ring is present on the top of the pan and bucket, illustrated by both Keen and Woolfenden, and a hole is present on this specimen.   The handles illustrated in Keen and Woolfenden are similar to two of those found at this site, one matching the lid diameter, the other for a lid 5" in diameter.   Both wire handles are 1/8" in diameter. While no handle rings are present on the dump specimens, the edge is deteriorated in places where they may have been situated. An alternative explanation for this item is a stove pipe hole cover.   A handle with looped ends also was recovered.

Remnants of a shallow pan were found at the main dump. The edges are reinforced by rolling the sheet metal around a thin wire. According to Jim Rock (personal communication 1985) the process started at least in the 1860s, if not before.

The possible edge of a shallow, cast iron pan with a tapered ring base was removed from the main dump.   The lip is flattish and slightly flanged (Fig.10c).   Similar examples are reported from Butte County sites (Tordoff and Maniery 1986:1-38, 1-39).

Fragmentary remains of a large, rolled-wire square pan are also evident at this site.   Alternatively, the wire remnants have been bent to form right angles after partial deterioration.

The fragmentary remains of a fluted-edge tin was recovered in the main deposit area (Fig. 15g). This may be a tart pan or equivalent.

Other miscellaneous metal containers (or parts thereof) include the zinc remnants of a Maltese cross-decorated screw cap to a Mason jar (Fig. 12b) (similar to those illustrated in Berge 1980:Fig. 59), and a hand-fabricated pipe elbow (Fig. 13a). Such a heavy piece may have been utilized in water control, as in a monitor. It was found on the

FIGURE 11

Tin lever-lid, possible top to a pan or lard bucket.

FIGURE 11

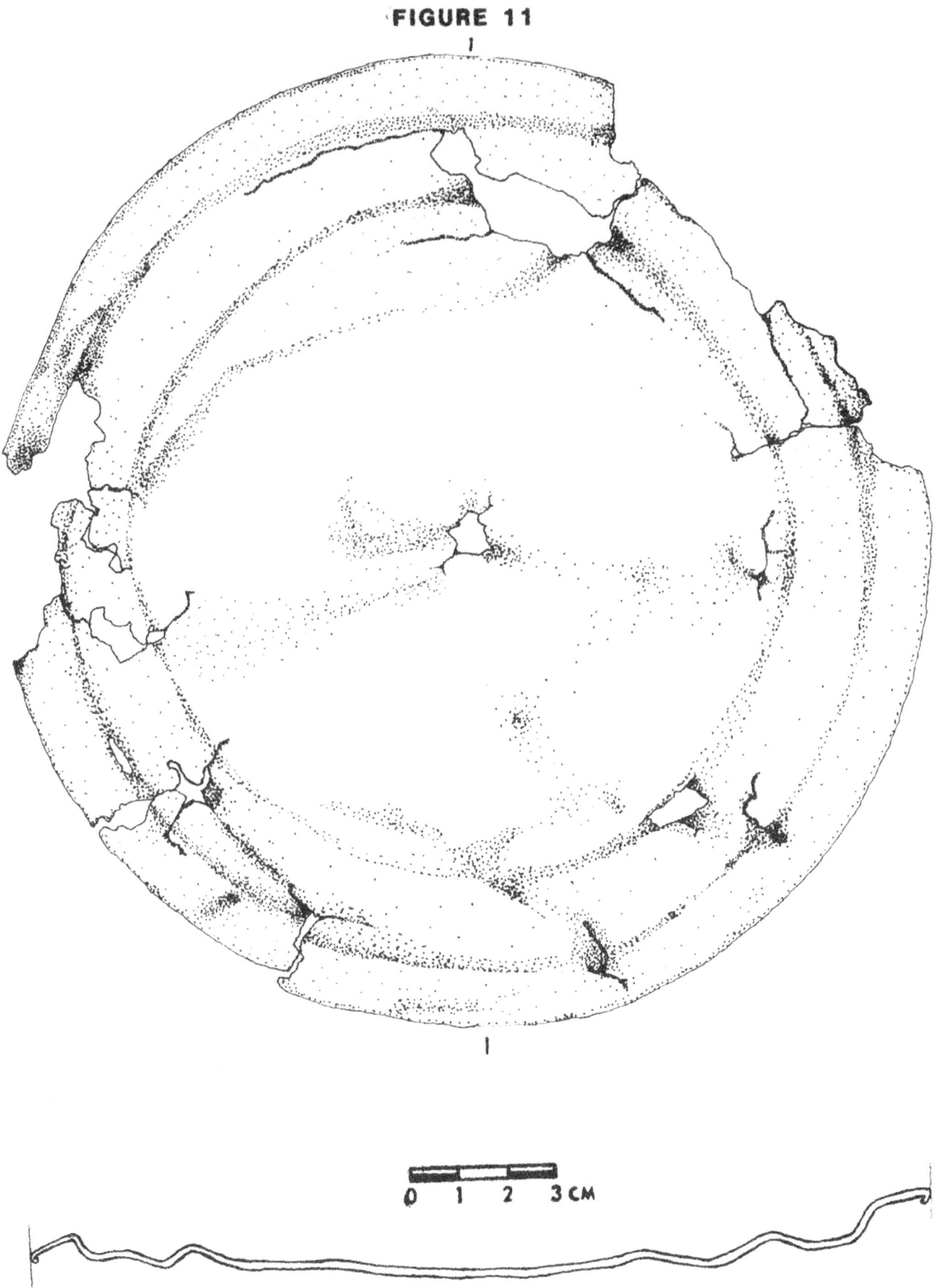

0 1 2 3 CM

surface near the dumps. Similarly, in the site area were noted a cut section of a sheet metal, riveted water pipe 18" in diameter and a metal band and bolt pipe coupler of the same diameter.

The former specimen exhibits missing sections cut out for use on other apparatuses. The latter coupler, composed of two riveted sections, has four rivet bolt attachments with 11/16" bolt holes. Such pipes were common in water control, as in hydraulic mining. These were obviously re-used for other purposes.

A flattened tin bucket with a twisted wire handle and wire reinforced rim, and a modified section of a galvanized bucket were encountered in the northerly dump area. The flattened cut side section of a bucket has near the lip two crossed ferrous strips attached with square and truss-headed ferrous rivets (Fig. 13b). Wire has been attached to one end of a band through a hole. This trapezoidal piece of bucket may have served as a small gate on a ditch outlet.

Next to the main dump was noted a squashed coffee pot. An embossed double band encircles the upper body. The handle was attached with malleable iron, tinned kettle ears. The lid is missing, although perhaps the earlier discussed lid belongs with this pot.

Axe Head

Downhill (easterly) of the reservoir was found a hand-forged single bit felling axe head since split longitudinally along the blade where it had been previously annealed (Fig. 14). According to Hull (1981:158-165) this is of the Ohio style (also see Fike and Phillips 1984:40-41). The poll exhibits considerable peening, as if the axe-head had been later used for a wedge. Such axes were manufactured from the 1820s until today (Russell 1967:262-263). Measurements for this artifact and the next grouping of metal artifacts are presented in Table 6.

Screwdriver and Other Tools

A screwdriver bit was recovered in the main dump (Fig. 15b). Three other flattened end bits 1/8" in diameter may be the ends of screwdrivers or a similar tool.

Another remnant of a probable mining-related tool is a metal band binding from the end of a pick handle nearest the pick head (Fig. 12e). It probably was used to reinforce the handle. The band has two holes, one of which is riveted. This was found in the main dump area.

Wire

Thirteen pieces of 12-1/2 gauge wire were recovered in the main dump. These pieces include straight, looped, hooked and twisted segments (Fig. 15h). A heavy irregular wire loop was observed on the site surface.

A used rivet was found in the main dump (Fig. 15c).

TABLE 6

Miscellaneous Metal Artifacts' Measurements*

Artifact	Length/Height	Diameter/Width	Thickness/Depth
Axe head	6-1/2	4-1/2	
poll	3-1/2	ca. 1-1/4	
Screwdriver bit	4		3/16
Pick handle binding	3-1/2	1-5/8	1/8
holes		7/16	
Wire (13)	1 - 6		1/16
Irregular wire loop	22	12	3/16
Rivet	1		3/16
Pot hanger	5-1/8		1/8
Pot hanger	6		1/8
Cutlery remnant	2-1/2	1/2	
Bands or straps (21)	1/2 - 31	1-1/4 (8)	1/16 (20)
		7/8 (5)	
		5/8 (4)	
		1 (2)	
		1-1/2 (2)	1/8
Stove pipe	24+	5	1/32
Shovel shank	9-1/2		
rivets (3)	1-1/2	1/2	
Copper sheathing	1-1/2	1/2	ca. 1/64

*All measurements in inches

57

FIGURE 12

a. Purple glass top to food jar (238-83).

b. Zinc remnants of a cross patee decorated screw cap to a Mason jar (238-115).

c. Lid to a fish (?) tin with key impression (238-112).

d. Possible s-twisted wire pot hanger (238-104).

e. Metal band binding from a probable pick handle (238-114).

FIGURE 12

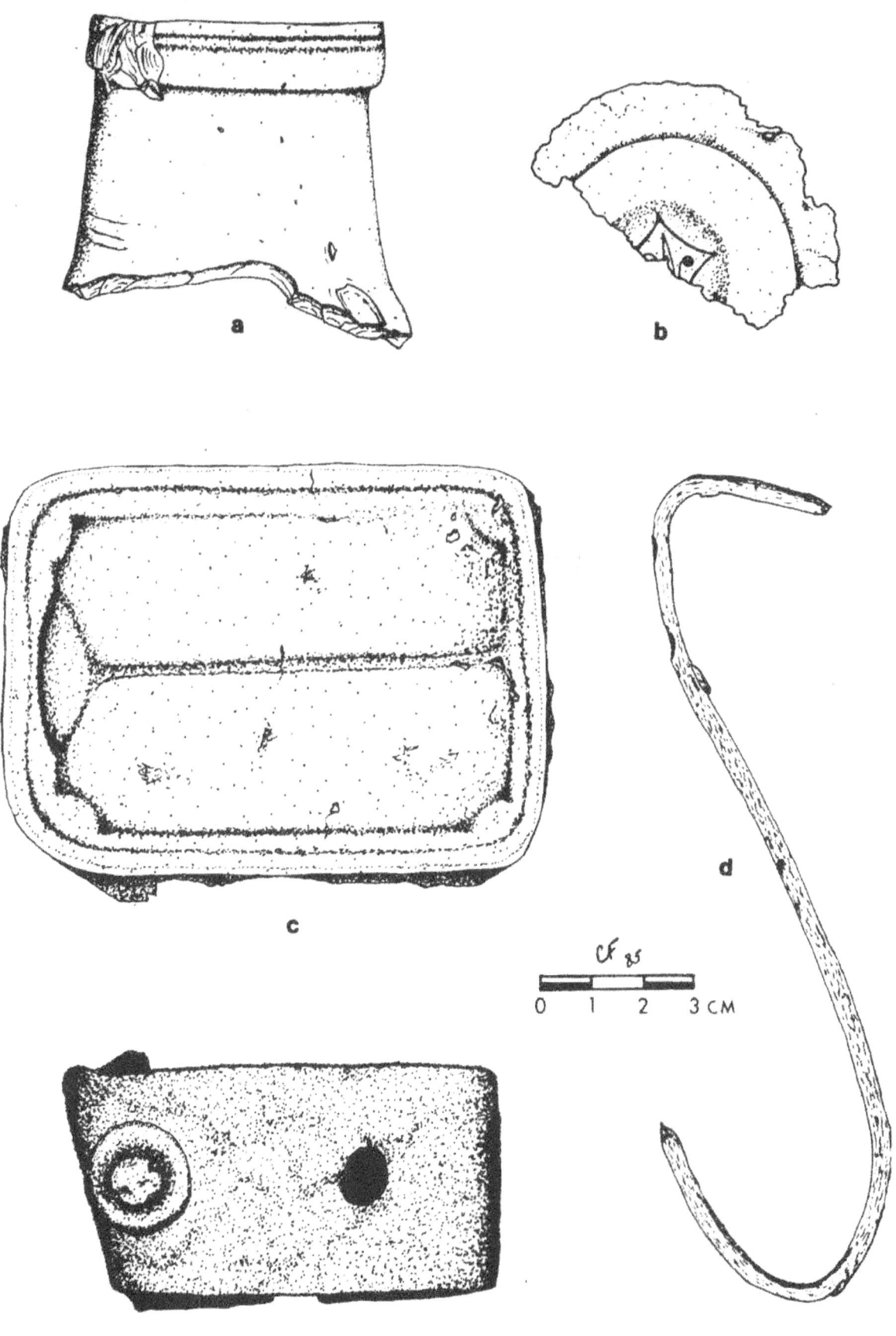

a

b

c

d

e

CF 85

0   1   2   3 CM

FIGURE 13

a.   Hand fabricated pipe elbow probably for water conveyance (238-92).

b.   Modified bucket (cut and flattened section) with attached metal bands (238-91).

FIGURE 13

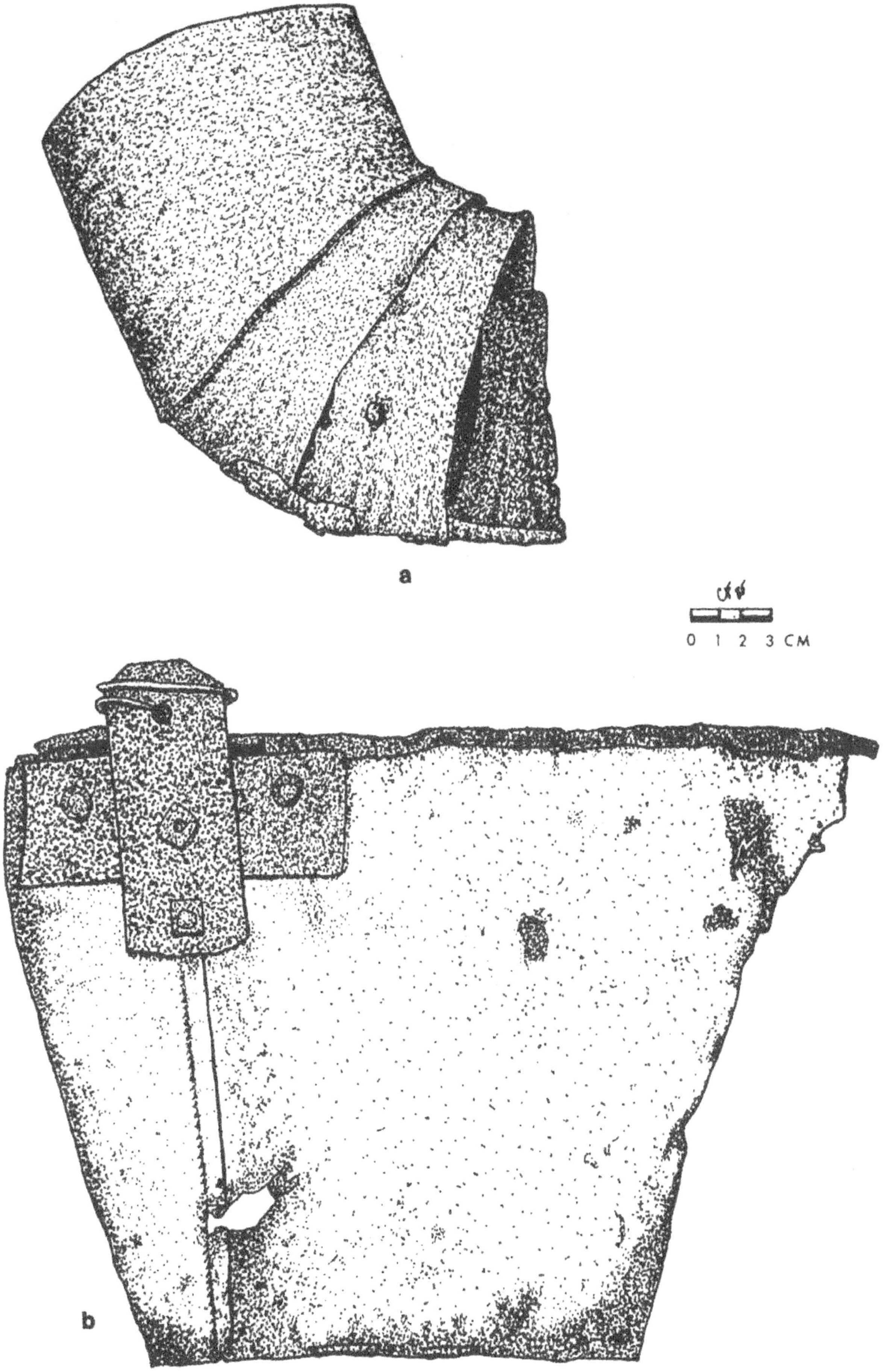

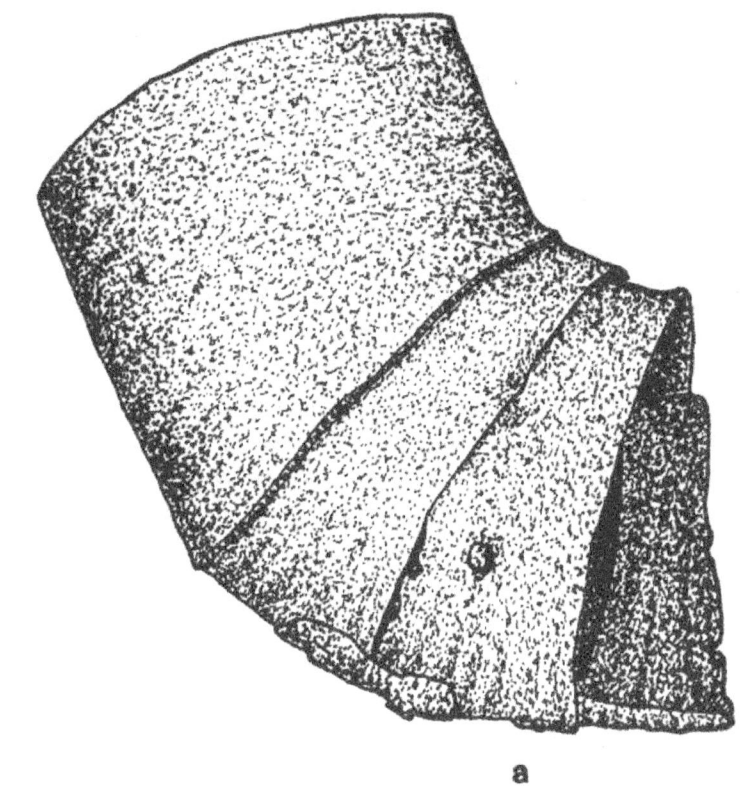

a

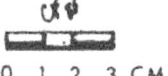

0 1 2 3 CM

b

FIGURE 14

Single bit felling axe split with the poll exhibiting considerable
peening (238-93).

FIGURE 14

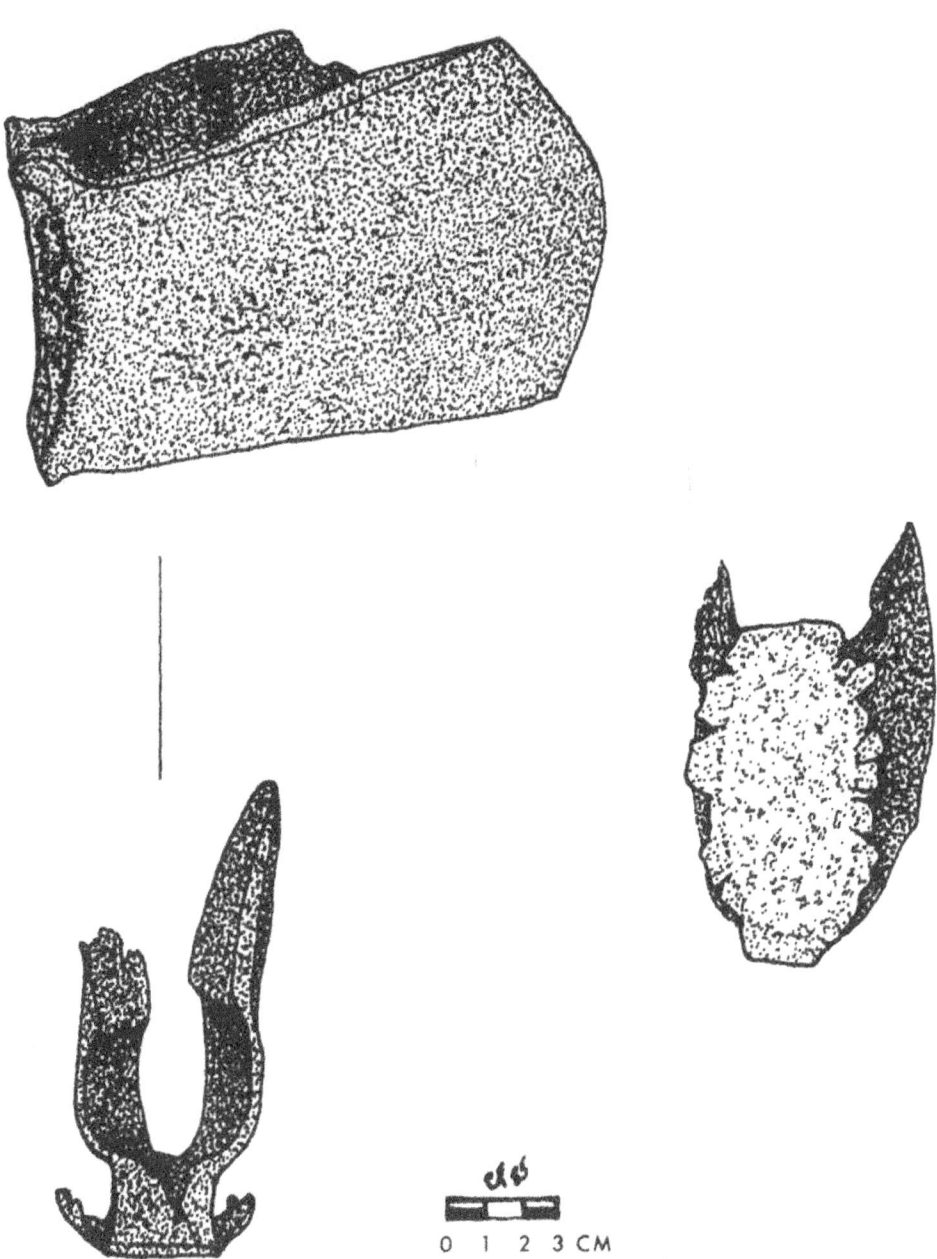

FIGURE 15

a. Cutlery handle remnant with studs (238-104).

b. Screwdriver bit or similar tool (238-105).

c. Rivet (238-106).

d. Copper sheathing of unknown function (238-101).

e. Brass shotgun shell casing, No. 12, New Rival Winchester brand (238-103).

f. Probable wire handle for pan or bucket (238-110).

g. Possible tart pan portion exhibiting fluted edge (238-99).

h. Twisted wire (12 1/2 gauge) (238-100).

FIGURE 15

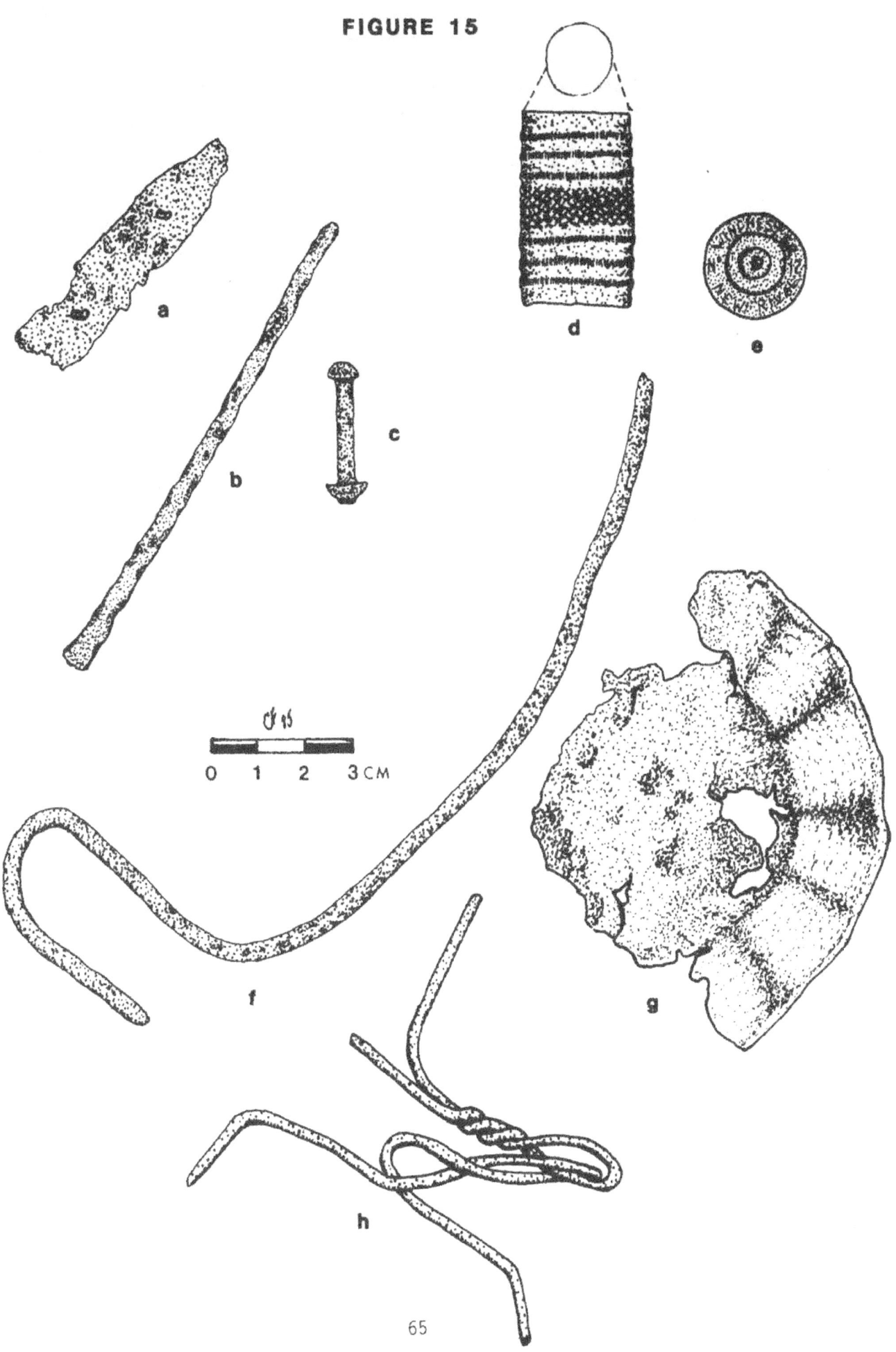

Two artifacts, of thick, S-twisted wire, which must have functioned as pot hangers, were recovered at the main dump (Fig. 15d).

The last metal artifact in this category is the handle remnant of a piece of cutlery (Fig. 15a). Two studs or rivets remain which originally held the bone or wood handle in place.

Bands or Straps

Portions of 21 metal bands, strips or straps were found within the main dump or scattered in a large area around the dump (see Table 6). One band has a second strip riveted on for reinforcing. Another of these strips (31" long) appears hinged at the center, also with riveted strips, for joining lengths together. Of two one-inch wide bands, one is folded into a Z and the other one is looped on the ends to form a handle. Two bands include one strip joined with another with a rivet for support.

Some of these bands might have been used on barrels and many undoubtedly functioned in the composition of mining equipment or mining related features.

Stove Pipe

Four rolled and riveted sections of probable stove pipe were found along the edge of the main dump also adjoining the low cobble rock wall. These sections are composed of sheet metal (see Table 6).

Shovel Shank

The ferrous shank portion of a shovel head was found in the main dump. The shank section is composed of two joining segments which were attached to the wooden handle by three rivets (see Table 6).

Copper Sheathing

A flattened piece of embossed copper sheathing was excavated from the principal dump (Fig. 15d). The embossing consists of a series of three rilled bands on each end with a wide cross-hatched diamond design band within the center. This sheath may have covered a small hose or other item.

AMMUNITION

The only indication of arms is the single brass shotgun shell casing recovered in the main dump area (Fig. 15e). This is a No. 12 New Rival Winchester shell which dates from 1901 into modern times according to Barnes (1965:288). This may be associated with the site's terminal use (Chinese occupation) sometime early after the turn of the century. Its incorporation in the dump debris suggests contemporaneous association.

FOOTWEAR PARTS

The rubberized heel and sole and rubberized insole fragments (with coarse, even-weave canvas fabrics attached) of a right shoe or boot were found within the main dump vicinity. These were not found together and could represent different items. These are probably parts of rubberized boots or gumboots, as reported by Tordoff and Maniery (1986:1-25, 1-26).

The heel is 2-11/16" in width and 2-3/4" in length. The insole is 2-3/4" wide, although it may be slightly contracted from its original size. None of these parts exhibit evidence of hobnails or of patching-repair.

DATING THE ASSEMBLAGE

The archival study of this site area clearly reflects mining-related use from about 1870 or earlier into the first decade of this century and later. Chinese activities near Igo seem to have come to an end during this latter time. The "Igo Chinese Workings" and associated living or activity area, the focus of this analysis, appear to have a more restricted period of use.

In examining the artifacts where there is some temporal control (Table 7) as related in the descriptive section, it would appear that the dominant site use, or at least use of the main dump area, occurred between ca. 1880 and 1905. This is in general accord with the documented use of this site area. What is interesting is the absence of firm dated artifacts manufactured only prior to 1882. This could suggest earlier use of this particular locus, and perhaps this site did not occur with earlier activities focused along Dry Creek or to the north at the Hardscrabble Mine, as documented. But, most likely, early periodic placering probably occurred at CA-Sha-1512 and artifactual evidence has been long removed by mining and other causes.

TABLE 7

Artifact Dating From The "Igo Chinese Workings"
(Major Period of Use)

Artifact	1850	1860	1870	1880	1890	1900	1910	1920	1930
Four Flowers Bowl									
Kuang Xu Seal				-----	-----	-----	-----		
Bamboo Bowls Only	-----	-----	-----	-----					
James Edward & Son Mark	-----	-----	-----						
Knowles-Taylor Mark			-----	-----	-----				
Grindley Mark				-----	-----	-----	-----	-----	-----
Cochran Mark				-----	-----	-----	-----		
Port Dundas Mark				-----	-----	-----	-----	-----	
Purple Glass Items			-----	-----	-----	-----	-----		
Window Glass Thickness			-----	-----					
Turn Mold Bottles			-----	-----	-----	-----			
Automated Machine Bottle						-----	-----	-----	-----
Applied Bottle Lips	-----	-----	-----	-----	-----	-----			
Fruit Jar (ground rim)	-----	-----	-----	-----					
Machine Cut Nails	-----	-----	-----	-----	-----	-----			
Wire Nails					-----	-----	-----	-----	-----
Key-wind Rectangular Tin						-----	-----	-----	-----
Hand Soldered Tin Cans	-----	-----	-----	-----					
Patched Holes in Tins	-----	-----	-----	-----	-----				
Wire Rim Tin--rolled	-----	-----	-----	-----	-----	-----			
New Rival Winchester						-----	-----	-----	-----
Shotgun Shell									

FAUNAL REMAINS

Faunal remains recovered from the main dump were identified by Dr. Peter Schulz of the California Department of Parks and Recreation. They consist of a pig (Sus scrofa) phalanx, two rib fragments, possibly pig, four plastron fragments of a Pacific pond turtle (Clemmys marmorata) and three unidentifable scraps. Such animals are not atypical for historic Chinese sites (cf. LaLande 1981:241-247).

DISCUSSION

Each of the research questions posed at the beginning of this report can now be addressed (in the order presented) to the extent the data permit. This approach provides a useful mechanism for contributing to the development of a model of rural Chinese mining life and external connections.

1. The first question relates to distinguishing Chinese from Euro-American mining activities and cross-fertilization of practices. The association of Chinese goods and archival data provide the main means of distinguishing--or at least identifying--site ethnic affiliation. LaLande (1981:333) found that in the Siskiyou Mountains of Oregon the tools and methods for mining differed little, if at all, from those employed by the Euro-Americans; that for the most part borrowing from the Euro-Americans was the order. Hardesty and Hattori (1984:3) arrived at a similar conclusion for the Cortez and Cornucopia mining camps in Nevada. This appears to be the case near Igo as well. It is well-documented that water control practices were already well-known to the Chinese who immigrated to California. There is some uncertainty, however, regarding the earthen reservoir origins and further research into their ultimate derivation (Chinese or otherwise) might prove promising.

2. The second question is how Chinese mining practices and support activities vary chronologically within the region and what relationships these practices or patterns have in a broader perspective.

    It would appear that around Igo/Piety Hill a number of Chinese during the 1850s to 1860s associated themselves formally or informally with large Euro-American run operations, settling in the main town. Such association is not meant to imply the Chinese did not have their own companies. Subsequently, and perhaps not until some of these large operations were shut down by hydraulic mining anti-debris laws did they venture out into their own "major" operations, as in the 1880s and 1890s. It cannot be ruled out, however, that such operations were simply part of a mining continiuum but with major white operations waning. One such operation was the "Igo Chinese Workings", probably the Schuyler Mine, listed as owned by a "Chinese Company".

    Comparison of the "Igo Chinese Workings" with those in the nearby Cottonwood Creek area reported by Johnson and Theodoratus (1984), Tordoff (1986), and Seldner (1986) suggest similar histories and patterns. Only fluvial deposits in the Cottonwood Creek tributaries necessitated more intense drainage placering in comparison to the Igo hydraulic operations. Ground-sluicing operations were common throughout the region within the domain of both Chinese and Euro-American miners. Apparent quartz hardrock mining by the Chinese at the Schuyler Mine may be unusual for the Chinese based on archival information (see LaLande 1981:322). Hardesty and Hattori (1983:4), on the other hand, mention Chinese hardrock miners in the Cortez mining district in Nevada. And Chiu (1963:33-34) notes that some Chinese were employed in the quartz mines in the central Sierra Nevada. Little or no record exists of individual Chinese claims, although this may be as much the product of poor records as actual practice. In a broader perspective, the current work of Seldner (1986) and Tordoff (1986) provides the best comparative documentation.

The similarities of the Igo operation with those reported in the Siskiyou Mountains in southern Oregon by LaLande (1981; 1985) are striking. In contrast, the operations in Trinity County (Kelly and McAleer 1985) and some in the Sierra Nevada (Felton et al. 1979) appear to be more labor intensive, often less removed from the larger urban centers with sizeable Chinese populations. The major difference between the Cottonwood-Igo operation and the others was in the seasonality of operation. That in the Sierra Nevada was more summer-fall oriented, a time when flooding was abated. In the Cottonwood-Igo area with its lower rainfall, increases in the fluvial regimes were not as extreme and the water was welcomed for the placering and hydraulicking (Smith 1983:5). This, of course, cross-cut ethnic boundaries. Seldner (1986) found archival evidence of large ditches providing water for year-round mining in the Cottonwood mining area.

It would seem that the Chinese population of Piety Hill rapidly decreased by the 1880s and the Chinese appear to have become involved in mining areas, as at CA-Sha-1512, peripheral to the earlier major claims or reworking older claims, a practice not new. At this same time in the nearby Cottonwood Creek area, census data (1880) indicate white and Indian populations were up and that there were still many, if not more, Chinese (Judith Tordoff, personal communication 1986). It is possible that many Piety Hill Chinese residents moved a few miles away to the better overall "diggings" at this time in this Cottonwood area.

3. The nature of Chinese subsistence at the site appears to be quite traditional, judging primarily from the ceramic vessels present and the few faunal remains (see LaLande 1981:336). This is in accord with the data recovered by Tordoff (1986) for the nearby Gas Point-Cottonwood area, and is the pattern found at Chinese sites throughout the west. One shotgun shell remnant might suggest limited hunting of local game with American armaments near the end of Chinese tenure in the region (cf. LaLande 1981:244 for a similar proposition). The presence of Euro-American liquor bottles and food jars suggests some accommodation for available products which may have been less expensive or more available than Chinese equivalents. This pattern is also not unique to Igo (cf. LaLande 1981:94; Felton et al. 1984:86-87). What is surprising is the absence of medicine bottles, part of the Chinese pattern of product use (Blanford 1986). This may be an outcome of site use (work environment trash versus primary living area trash) or substitution (liquor over patent medicine).

The relative frequencies and types of Chinese ceramics (Table 1) says much with regard to the economic status of the miners, site dating, and subsistence practices. Sando and Felton (1984) found records from one area that indicate Double Happiness and Bamboo bowls were considerably cheaper than Winter Green or Four Season bowls, the former being valued at one-half of the latter. By the 1870's the Bamboo bowls were far more prevalent than the Double Happiness bowls (Felton et al. 1984:94). As Double Happiness bowls are absent at the Igo site, we can probably assume it post-dates 1870 (and is predominantly later yet). Brott (1982:54) does not see this pattern where family units resided, apparently not the case here.

The relative frequency of the cheaper to more expensive ceramics and the ceramic types is informative. In comparing Winter Green-Four Seasons to Bamboo vessels, we see there are 15 of the former to seven of the latter, a better than 2:1 ratio. Of course, many of the former types are small soup spoons or cups which, if discounted, would give a nearly 1:1 ratio. Still, the presence of so many expensive vessels implies either a heavier level of investment or availability and perhaps a locally stable living situation as suggested by Felton et al. (1984:96). But, it appears most likely, as Felton et al. (1984:96) state: "Since the cheaper wares occurred only as rice bowls, poor immigrants (rural miners) who lived in stable situations would no doubt have invested in Winter Green or Four Flower ceramics to meet their needs for other vessel varieties." The situation at the "Igo Chinese Workings" is no doubt comparable to the coeval table setting of Berkeley truck farm workers pictured by Jaffa (1901:pl. 1) where Bamboo bowls were in use with Four Flowers serving bowls.

Where ferrous artifacts are concerned, the pattern is one of accommodation. Local Euro-American products were purchased or salvaged and often modified to fit the needs of local mining variance or for other use. There would appear outwardly to be little differentiation with Euro-American mining ventures. In the habitation area, most metal artifacts appear to reflect canned foods, oils, storage or carrying containers, tools for small-scale work, structure remains, cooking vessels or apparatuses, and items related to food preparation or consumption. Use of chopsticks probably accounts for the rarity of cutlery.

Based on preliminary results from the nearby Dutch Gulch area (Tordoff 1986) there does not appear to be much variation in subsistence/technology of the Chinese communities. Ginger jars are missing in the Dutch Gulch-Cottonwood assemblages as are food storage jars of American manufacture. This difference does not seem significant.

The archive sources suggest quite a bit of horticulture and some animal husbandry (ducks, etc.). However, mining and erosion and, perhaps, sample bias prevent any archaeological insights other than from the few faunal remains (turtle, pig) recovered at the site.

4.   The next research question addresses the interaction of Chinese and Euro-American commerce. It has been pointed out that a Chinese store was present at Piety Hill. One was also situated at Gas Point some five miles distant until 1911 and a store was located in the 1850-1860s at least at nearby Horsetown with white and Chinese goods (Judith Tordoff, personal communication 1985). These outlets were along the main stage route up Dry Creek (Johnson and Theodoratus 1984:260), one of the main routes between Red Bluff (the terminus of steam ships) and the main settlements of Shasta and Weaverville to the north and west (Beauchamp 1973:6). It would seem that there was ready accessibility to Chinese goods from suppliers. Hanover (1982:11) notes that in Trinity County, at an early date, they even had their own pack train to bring in supplies. Furthermore (1982:17), she states that "...Chinese trade was very considerable. Teams were unloading for them every day or two."

White stores in Igo were also readily available to users of the site region, at least by the 1880s. Assuming Chinese use of the site, Euro-American goods (aside from liquor) were being purchased or acquired and used (and modified) in the place of, or as supplements to, traditional goods. Here we include some of the vitrified white earthenware cups, plates and bowls and metal tins containing such items as fish or meat and other goods, a metal coffee pot, Mason jars, etc. An examination of Table 8 shows a comparison of Chinese and Euro-American glass and ceramic containers and tableware. Almost certainly there always was a reliance on mining-oriented equipment of Euro-American manufacture, although, as noted, considerable re-fabrication or modification is apparent. LaLande (1981:328) notes that in the Applegate Valley of Oregon shovels, picks, galvanized buckets, axes and hatchets were common purchases by the Chinese from white merchants. Such items were quite evident at the "Igo Chinese Workings". Mary Maniery of Public Anthropological Research in Sacramento (personal communication 1986) has a list of purchases made by Chinese at Dempsey Store near Somes Bar on the Klamath River during the 1860s-1870s that included shovels, picks, and other Anglo tools. Chinese occupants, perhaps as much for maintaining good relations as for need, seemed to have used both Chinese and white merchants. Greenway (1985:6) notes that isolation factors may account for mixed Chinese - Euro-American assemblages.

5.   The probable social and economic relationships between the Chinese and non-Chinese miners and the effects of these relationships on activities on the land through time have been touched upon in previous discussions.

It seems apparent that the Chinese in relatively large numbers were hired early-on by local major mining companies like the Dry Creek Tunnel and Flume Company for ditch construction,

Table 8

Containers - Tableware (glass-ceramic)

	Beverage	Shipping/ Storage	Food Service/ Consumption	Food Preparation	Totals
Chinese	2	8	22		32
Euro-American	15*	3*	5		23
Unknown				1	1
Totals	17	11	27	1	56

* Glass

75

probably reservoir construction, and mining directly, especially where hard labor was involved. Around Igo as the large white ventures curtailed or as the high grade deposits were exhausted, the Chinese locally, possibly in relatively small groups or companies and maybe in conjunction with more influential Chinese companies--as in San Francisco, began working marginal areas or areas where the hydraulic debris could be controlled (e.g. consider the Wing Yuen Co. agreement).

LaLande (1981:324-325) has noted that due to legal restrictions on ownership, the Chinese generally did not file claims themselves, but rather had a local white do it for them, and then they would purchase the claim from this agent, providing a more secure deed in this manner (also see Shay 1876:156 and Seward 1881:48). Such a practice has probably obscured the true extent of Chinese mining practices in the region. The Schuyler Mine, the apparent center of this study, is possibly a case in point of re-purchase. The fact that there exist 80 acres of unpatented public land with clear evidence of Chinese use may be a reflection of legal restrictions on the Chinese, but more likely simply reflects no need for such an action by the operators relative to gold output, as has occurred for years on many public land parcels.

There is little record of hostilities between the Chinese and non-Chinese in the Igo area, although records from other regions of Shasta County suggest there were unfriendly encounters, certainly racial biases, and antipathy (cf. DuFault 1959:156-157; Chiu 1963:18-19; Johnson and Theodoratus 1984:256). The community separation (Igo-Piety Hill) probably reflects not only ethnic solidarity but protectiveness as well. Toward Gas Point during the height of the hydraulic mining (circa 1860s-1870s) era, white farmers expressed hostility toward the Chinese miners (Johnson and Theodoratus 1984:267-268), but at least one record of water right agreements (mentioned earlier) indicates cooperation between a farming family and a Chinese company by the end of the 19th century. The archaeological remains suggest very late mining operations by Chinese who appear to have purchased some Euro-American goods, probably because it was expedient, but also perhaps to relieve the antipathy and tension between the groups.

6. Interactions between the local (Piety Hill) and urban Chinese were probably long standing (cf. Smith 1983:4). A trade network for economic goods, primarily those related to subsistence, leisure, and day-to-day living, was evidently in order from the early 1850s. The main node was centered in San Francisco with a major artery extending through the Igo-Piety Hill area to Shasta and Weaverville and points beyond. This network may have been later expanded into corporate financing for Chinese-owned mining ventures such as the Schuyler operation.

As the Chinese population declined in the Igo-Piety Hill and other areas by the late 1880s and 1890s and the corresponding demand for Chinese goods lessened, this network, as a result, changed with possibly different suppliers (as at Gas Point?) at a more sporadic interval. This may explain the use of some Euro-American ceramics and glass as tableware and food storage containers. It would seem that those Chinese who left the area as the mines declined eventually moved into the urban centers to the south, like Sacramento and San Francisco.

7.   This question, related to resource competition, racial bias, and/or social organization of the Chinese miners and other groups with regard to settlement/activity patterning, has been addressed in part in the previous answers. There are only a few comments to be added.

Piety Hill, the main local settlement, was virtually abandoned by the white population as hydraulic mining loomed closer and the nearby town of Igo was founded. The Chinese, already established as a community in Piety Hill, decided to stay on, perhaps due to the expense of moving, but also probably due to the desire to maintain the Chinese identity established and to provide a buffer with the white community which probably did not want them in Igo in any case. As it turned out, the Chinese foresight not to move proved accurate (or luck prevailed) as mining never did reach Piety Hill. It is also evident that some Chinese lived or carried out food preparation-consumption activities next to their mining ventures and related structure(s), a short distance from the community, at least during the last two decades or so of the 19th century and the first few years of the 20th century. This would seem to be the case at the site under study.

8.   With respect to seasonality of use, the Igo data do nothing to refute Johnson and Theodoratus' (1984:267) statement that "there is no documentary evidence that the Chinese left the area in the off season." In fact, the size and probable complexity of the local community and the census data suggest year round occupation. The earlier citation regarding mining with ditch waters for 10 months of the year, (although more restricted in the drier months), suggests there would be little need for all to leave, and summer agriculture and preparation for the next season probably filled some voids.

9.   The differences between Chinese mining and settlement at Igo-Piety Hill, Dutch Gulch-Cottonwood and other areas of northern California, at a distance from the main commercial centers with Chinese communities, are not apparent. The transportation-trade network overcame distance and, seemingly, remoteness except during the earliest time of use and when the Chinese population was vastly diminished. It might be that activities (certainly settlements) at Igo-Piety Hill were more nucleated--perhaps owing to the nature of the gold-bearing beds--than at the nearby Gas Point District. Activities-settlement at the Gas Point vicinity nearby generally may have

77

been more ephemeral, more spread out owing to the more dispersed nature of the auriferous beds (cf. Smith 1983). This, of course, does not mean to imply that major operations were not present, as along Cottonwood Creek. Smith (1983:5) notes that "the number, variability and associations of individual features of many project area site complexes suggest the presence of a structured company or companies of miners."

10. Discussion regarding differences in the Chinese-Euro-American mining activities in the Igo-Dutch Gulch-Cottonwood area and elsewhere in California-Oregon has been briefly touched upon previously. Johnson and Theodoratus (1984:367) have noted that theories or hypotheses regarding Chinese and Euro-American mining systems would be premature. Until they can be distinguished archaeologically or ethnohistorically, this study can add little. LaLande (1981:310-334; 1985:29) offers numerous comments along this line.

    It seems clear that the water available for mining in the Igo-Dutch Gulch-Cottonwood area was less than within many of the Sierran and other Klamath Mountain mining districts. Still, the elaborate ditch network allowed extensive, probably for much of the year, hydraulic mining at selected mines. Booming, as described by Hammond (1890:122), probably also occurred. The gate mechanism recovered at the "Igo Chinese Workings" may be indicative of this technique, a situation where the water supply was somewhat diminished. Tordoff (1986) offers worthwhile comparisons in her more extensive study noting the marginality of many of the Dutch Gulch-Cottonwood operations in comparison to other areas of California where much water and rich gravels often provided for extensive and extended mining except during the rainy winter season, a time of extensive activities on the west side of the Valley around Igo-Dutch Gulch. Judith Tordoff (personal communication 1986) believes the Dutch Gulch-Cottonwood Chinese mining may have been quite different than near Igo, since the former had no hardrock mining, only placer, a condition which favored more individualistic, labor-intensive mining concerns. This may be true in the general sense, but in the site vicinity there seems to have been limited drift mining, most attention being paid to the ancient gravels and more recent alluvium.

11. The relationship between Chinese mining techniques and those in the homeland are generally beyond the scope of this study. LaLande (1981:323) notes "The Chinese excelled at feeding their claims with numerous ditches, part of their heritage of irrigated agriculture in Kwangtung." Certainly, ditch construction and use (as among the Euro-American miners) was the forte of the "Igo Chinese Workings" workers.

12. The next question regarding differences in the productivity of Chinese as opposed to white operations is not readily definable with the information at hand. The lateness of operations like the Schuyler suggests a willingness not shared by white-owned

companies to pursue moderate-sized ventures and exert necessary controls (debris dams, etc.) on apparent marginal deposits. But even this trend was relatively short lived.

From an overall gold production point of view, it is very doubtful if any of the Chinese operations could match the output of the Hardscrabble Mine. This extensive working certainly made use of Chinese labor, and some Chinese groups, initially lacking capital backing, probably stayed affiliated with the Dry Creek Tunnel and Flume Company or others for some time--perhaps into the 1880s--before venturing into their own hydraulic operations. Another reason for this lateness was probably due to the white control of available water. Thus, Chinese operations until late were possibly quite limited, labor-intensive, and very seasonal relying on winter run-off. Furthermore, LaLande (1985:44) notes that conical pits, as observed at the CA-Sha-1512 site, when still visible indicate areas of low mineral potential, at least by 19th century standards.

13. The magnitude of the "Igo Chinese Workings" suggests a well-controlled and integrated operation. This operation, owing to its close proximity to a Chinese settlement (Piety Hill), may not have included a major work camp but rather a small one consisting of several individuals only, perhaps mine overseers and/or ditch and reservoir tenders. More workers could have come from the local town daily leaving behind at the site a few watchmen (and their daily trash) when they returned home. The overall operation would seem to be that of one company, although from a broader perspective there appear to be links (ditch connections, reservoir similarities) with operations up Dry Creek, in the vicinity of the Hardscrabble Mine, and further down Dry Creek. Whether these were synchronous does not appear evident in all cases, and, in fact, the ditch to the site in question was plugged in order to supply water to the up-stream operation. However, this could easily have been changed on a daily basis. Either directly or indirectly (i.e. through merchants, tax collectors, etc.) there was probably communication regarding the activities of neighboring miners and operations. Whether such communications fostered cooperation between companies is uncertain. That earlier mining occurred in the vicinity is evident from the shallow gullies and scattered surface cobbles resulting from ground sluicing, no doubt at an early time in the mining history, judging from superimposed features.

14. A likely explanation for the site's artifact patterning lies in the dismantling and possible salvaging of a building, and the general cleanup of the remains and disposal in the adjoining low ditch, the location possibly of several episodes of earlier disposal. Judgment for this conclusion is derived from the dump contents and juxtaposition to several features possibly representing structure foundations.

The nails and window glass, door knob, stove pipe remains and possible foundation stones suggest a small structure, such as a house or work shed. LaLande's (1981:304) description from the

Siskiyous seems to fit: "The structures...were probably simple cabins with vertical siding, plank or shake roofs, and small windows..." Hardesty and Hattori (1984:4) note that in the Cortez and Cornocopia mining districts of Nevada where there were large Chinese communities, the structures apparently built and used by the Chinese utilized much of the same design techniques and raw materials as in the Euro-American settlements.

The main area of non-mining use, as mentioned, was Piety Hill. Trails on aerial photos between this town and the reservoir area are evident as is a road to Igo not far beyond. So, while mining-related activities (food preparation and consumption, some opium smoking, and mining-related labor) were carried out at the site by a few Chinese (most likely men), other activities centered on commerce, entertainment, politics, social integration, etc. were available to them in close proximity. The presence of opium-smoking paraphernalia at the site is not surprising. This was a common practice among the Chinese as discussed in Felton et al. (1984:98-107). In a hard-work mining operation, opium use was no doubt tied to relief from strenuous working conditions or illness. In reference to Piety Hill, Ballou notes (1954:20): "In those days opium smoking was carried on openly, and I have seen many Chinese lying on their reed mats with a wooden block for a pillow twirling a bit of opium on a wire over a little lamp, then putting it into the bowl of a large bamboo pipe, and smoking it."

The absence of decorative items, game pieces, coins, medicine vials, large storage vessels, fancy wares, and other items supports the notion of more ephemeral, sporadic activities or limited habitation. While other activity areas are probably present in the vicinity, it is hard to explain the relative absence of faunal remains. Preservation factors can be discounted owing to the presence of several intact bones. Food trash may have been disposed elsewhere, as in the nearby depression. There also does not appear to be a great deal of trash to support intense or long-term habitation or use. One other point: Toward the end of site occupation there was an apparently rapid decline in the Chinese population--and probably goods and services--at Piety Hill.

Within the site itself the occupation-use refuse is highly localized. Other artifacts scattered about the site are directly related to mining or correspond to liquor consumption (or at least bottle disposal). The trash dump areas equate generally with LaLande's (1981:117) site activity areas at Gin Lin's Camp at "Little Applegate Diggings". LaLande (1981:117) suggests his areas probably represent the former sites of living quarters with associated cooking/eating areas. It is possible that no occupation occurred at the site, only daytime activities associated with mining and mid-day meals. Absence of animal bone may thus be accounted for by consumption of secondary mid-day meals relying more heavily on soups and rice than meat. There are also few food cans and cooking utensils which might support this notion.

In comparing the Igo and Dutch Gulch-Cottonwood Chinese use patterns, there appear to be differences. In the Dutch Gulch-Cottonwood area, most Chinese mining sites are very ephemeral, containing one or more hearth features and scattered artifacts. "It is likely the people using them lived in tents and may have cooked outdoors" (Smith 1983, Johnson and Theodoratus 1984:66). These features were found in association with ditches and placer tailings and most were used from the 1860s through the 1880s (Johnson and Theodoratus 1984:66-67). A rammed-earth structure of probable Chinese origin was also found along with 30 sites with earthen dams, numerous ditches, pads, tailings, etc. The pattern of scattered, often re-used and re-fabricated mining-related metal artifacts is present, although certain Chinese associations are not often evident.

15. The next question relates to Euro-American influences on mining and non-mining related technology, subsistence, leisure and other facets of culture. The best evidence at the Igo-Piety Hill location is within the realm of technology-subsistence.

Felton et al. (1984:84-98) have presented a revealing discussion of ethnicity and the question of cultural conservativeness pertinent to this question. From a purely archaeological standpoint, the question of Chinese use needed to be first established at the site complex. Following the analysis of Felton et al. (1984:85-86), where there is a high rate of Chinese to Euro-American ceramics, the site can be attributable to Chinese occupants. Table 8 (discounting glass containers and not including opium pipe bowls or a teapot of questionable origin) reveals 84% of the ceramic vessels are Chinese. The ethnicity of the small habitation area and most likely the localized site as a whole seems established. This was more evident after examining archival sources.

The presence, frequency, and type of Euro-American ceramic vessels and glass bottles is in accord with numerous other Chinese sites in the West (cf. Felton et al. 1984:84-87). The acquisition of non-Chinese goods appears to be expedient. By and large it would seem that the local Chinese miners maintained as much of their native material culture and practices as possible, as LaLande (1981:337) found in southern Oregon under similar conditions. Adaptation of American mining techniques and technology by the Chinese was necessitated by conditions, availability of materials and an apparent lack of a well-established mining tradition of their own. However, mining was carried out in China from early times (cf. Bente and Smith 1984:8-9). As noted by LaLande (1981:337), "...the Chinese often 'made do' with whatever materials or housing was available to them, and then proceeded to modify it to their own needs (or as circumstances dictated)." With strong traditional values maintained over the years, the need for flexibility, adaptability and cooperation is all too evident. Still, in the realm of leisure, perhaps social networks, community organization, religion, economic structure and order, traditional behavior was apparently maintained to the extent possible so distant from the home base (cf. Hardesty and Hattori 1984:6).

16.   The next question deals with the matter of Chinese acculturation in the mining community, and is related closely to the previous question. Twenty to thirty years of contact with the dominant Euro-American culture no doubt had some effect on the culture of the Chinese occupants. Greenwood (1980:114), in discussing the Chinese in historic California, wonders "...whether the usual standards of acculturation even apply when there is neither opportunity nor advantage to adapting to the host culture." However, see Rusco and Hattori's (1986) recent discussion. It has been noted, as LaLande (1981:333) previously found, that the technological pattern of the Chinese miners behavior illustrates a high level of acculturation, that is adaptation or assimilation of Euro-American mining equipment and techniques for economic gain. But, in line with the question, there is no evidence to suggest much more than expediency rather than true cognitive changes. It would seem that Langenwalter's (1980:110) conclusion for a Chinese colony along the Fresno River associated with gold mining can be applied here: "Thus, no concrete demonstration of acculturation in the cognitive sense is evident. This indicates the scarcity of foodstuffs, intensity of intercultural contact, length of exposure or a combination of all were not exerting sufficient pressure to select for the acculturation of the traditional pattern."

The fact that the Chinese eventually left the Igo-Piety Hill area possibly reflects economic need, but also a reconsolidation of fragmented traditional communities into viable urban settings where the traditional life-style could be continued into the 20th century. Some probably returned to China.

17.   The relationship of adaptation, assimilation and acculturation to the "Sojourner's Thesis" was the next question presented. The thesis, in review, is that the Chinese immigrant of the 19th century came not to establish permanent residence in California, but to accumulate his earnings and return to China.

The data from the Igo-Piety Hill area only in a very general sense seem to agree with this thesis, especially for those who arrived earlier. Such an agreement is based on the evidence regarding acculturation and archival data. However, the census records, as previously indicated, show that a few lingered on for at least 20 to 30 years and probably longer, perhaps with no intention of returning. The corporate nature of the Schuyler operation near the turn of the last century suggests that a number of individuals associated with the mining venture were probably permanent Chinese-American residents (see Rusco and Hattori 1986).

18.   The correspondence of acculturation-assimilation among remnant Chinese at Piety Hill-Igo with the tail end of intensive-extensive mining and mining-related activities is difficult to assess with the data at hand. Stores offering Chinese goods

82

were still present to the end. It seems enough Chinese remained in the area through the turn of the century to maintain a continuity of tradition and a network of contacts. The possible corporate connection with San Francisco may have remained and travel to, and communication with, the urban centers with Chinese populations became easier near the waning years of the mining era. Because of the above, it appears even small groups of Chinese were able to cling to their homeland values despite adaptation to certain facets of Euro-American technology, subsistence, economy, and politics. The Exclusion Act may have had influence on local populations, but this was not fully explored in this study.

Thus, as best as can be determined, in good times and bad times, whether large or small Chinese and Euro-American populations were present, trade-shipment problems and so on do not seem to have exerted significant value changes on the local Chinese--merely changes in product use, housing or communal activities. It is likely, however, that some of those who remained into later years no longer intended to return to China.

19. The final question centers on the declining Chinese population, restrictions placed on mining, and declines in productive gold-bearing beds as an influence on corporate Chinese mining, and the scale of Chinese mining.

The nature of the "Igo Chinese Workings" suggests to this writer small corporate ventures into the 1890s with accommodations made for restrictive mining laws, possible discrimination, and declining availability of mining-related and other technology (hence perhaps the re-worked materials). However, marginal returns, low capital-income and simple expediency can account for the hand-made and re-fabricated mining-related artifacts.

Individualistic pursuits are not readily apparent, although no more than a few individuals occupied or worked the reservoir area. This may conform to Hardesty and Hattori's (1983:5) "sojourner" household. This is deceiving, however, since a known community of Chinese was very near at hand. The declining mining venture by the Chinese is in accord with that of the larger Euro-American population. Economic reasons, probably more than social, led to the eventual abandonment of the Igo/Piety Hill area by resident Chinese-Americans.

CONCLUSIONS

The recovered assemblage and features generally typify historic Chinese sites in the West and mining related sites in particular (cf. Evans 1980; LaLande 1981; Hardesty and Hattori 1984) with some minor differences. The relationship to the Chinese assemblages recovered from the nearby Dutch Gulch project are in general accord (Judith Tordoff, personal communication 1985). Both assemblages reflect ready access to commercial outlets supplying the day-to-day items of Chinese manufacture needed for traditional subsistence, storage, and consumption. Items expedient to mining enterprises and housing reflect scarcity and adaptation of Euro-American artifacts. Re-use, modification and adaptation are readily apparent.

No mining features can be ascribed 100% to Chinese traditions, but ditch work and earthen berm dam/reservoir construction likely had roots in China, a topic left for others to pursue.

The Chinese in the Igo-Piety Hill vicinity evidently established initial ties with large Euro-American mining concerns, becoming increasingly economically independent with time. However, this independence, a reflection of capital accumulation and/or investment from urban Chinese groups, was manifested in relatively small operations compared to those Euro-American ventures of an earlier time. Constraints regarding mining procedures and perhaps the marginal nature of the deposits may have similarly been limiting agents. It is also possible the Chinese were involved locally in draft mining, apparently not a very common practice.

The regional pattern of Chinese and Euro-American mining includes some diversity cross-cutting cultural boundaries. The area around Igo-Piety Hill was less marginal overall than nearby deposits around the Dutch Gulch-Cottonwood Creek-Gas Point area. Here at Piety Hill, the Chinese colony was more centralized and juxtaposed with a moderate-size white community with corresponding economic and even socio-political conveniences (both communities together providing stores, opium dens, community "centers", assay offices, etc.).

In addition, operations here were nearly year round, at least those able to tap into the principal ditches and reservoirs. Mining intensity, however, probably corresponded with rainfall-runoff. Despite these factors, the Chinese miners themselves were still relatively impoverished judging from the quality and types of traditional goods and the considerable re-working and substitution of metallic goods or contained goods.

It seems that the Igo-Piety Hill Chinese community was part of an expansive commercial network from early Gold Rush times into the 20th century. Still, this network probably expanded and then contracted as the gold fields and population declined. The area of activities was along one of the main trade arteries from the San Francisco-Sacramento nodes. During declining years, access to traditional goods by the Chinese was probably more sporadic, but this was counteracted by increased shipping-transportation efficiency.

The workings under consideration here were close at hand to the Piety
Hill community. This makes sense in terms of access. That these
Chinese claims were unproductive cannot be fully appraised, but
ongoing interest and later 20th century mining suggest value, but
probably difficulty in working without hydraulic systems and water
rights, or modern technology.

The Piety Hill Chinese community and the nearby Chinese workings and
habitation or support area most likely provided a buffer to white
claims and the white town of Igo nearby. This fact provided a means
for Chinese community-culture continuity and socio-political
integration. Chinese values were maintained while adaptation was
expedient and never cost-effective. Access to Euro-American goods
and services and a transportation network were right at hand. In the
end the few resident property owners probably re-trenched into urban
settings with Chinese colonies, probably as much as a self-defense
mechanism from the biased Euro-Americans as a desire for ethnic
solidarity and neo-traditional ways.

In a broader perspective and in general, the Chinese operations near
Piety Hill-Igo are most similar to those of this same time in nearby
Trinity County, Siskiyou County, northern Butte County, and southern
Oregon. This was due to similar environments (natural and cultural),
a similar communication-commercial network, and, apparently, a
similarity in ethnic links to China.

Greenwood (1982:246-251) has presented a discussion of models of
historic sites in the New Melones area of the Sierra Nevada as a
theoretical framework for learning. In her discussion she found that
a Victorian-Dependency Model most accurately explains the sites in
the Sierran drainage (Greenwood 1982:250). In this model, historic
development of a site or region and the archaeological remains can be
considered partially dependent on outside forces yet partially
self-sufficient.

This model applies to the "Igo Chinese Workings" and associated
Chinese settlement in its general or ideal sense. Certainly this was
not a static situation. At an early time (ca. 1850s to 1860s)
numerous Chinese workers, apparently individually or in groups,
depended on white miners for some revenue (earnings) and a supply and
communication line from commercial ports and urban Chinese centers
(San Francisco-Sacramento) providing traditional goods and
information. The Chinese may have been organized on the local level
with more-or-less self-sufficient labor groups with a go-between
Chinese foreman. By the 1870s, despite continued white racism,
until the turn of the century there was a measure of independence
among the local Chinese workers, including work companies, probable
social groups, a community, fresh food supplies (gardens), agents,
local merchants, etc., but with continued links to commercial and
informational lines to the distant urban centers, to China, and,
undoubtedly, links to Euro-American dominated companies with water
control and mining supplies. At the end, the few Chinese left, while
undoubtedly largely self-sufficient and "Americanized" to some

extent, lacked the social integrating institutions (cf. Greenwood 1980:119), the community necessary for maintaining an ethnic identity. This and probable continued discrimination led to a retrenchment back to urban centers with viable Chinese communities.

REFERENCES

Amory, Cleveland
   1969   The 1902 Edition of the Sears Roebuck Catalogue. Bounty Books, New York.

Andacht Sandra, Nancy Garthe and Robert Mascarelli
   1984   Price Guide to Oriental Antiques. Second Edition, Wallace - Homestead, West Des Moines.

Andrews, Alexander Robertson
   1964   Horsetown. The Covered Wagon. The Shasta County Historical Society Yearbook, pp. 3-11. Redding.

Ballou, R. S.
   1954   The Story of Igo. The Covered Wagon. The Shasta County Historical Society Yearbook, pp. 19-24. Redding.

Barnes, Frank C.
   1965   Cartridges of the World. Follet Publishing Company, New York.

Beauchamp, Jean Moores
   1973   Shasta: The Queen City. California Historical Society, San Francisco.

Bente, Vance G. and Mary Hilderman Smith
   1984   Cottonwood Creek Project, Shasta and Tehama Counties, California. Dutch Gulch Lake, An Evaluation of Selected Historic Archaeological Resources. Report Submitted to Theodoratus Cultural Research, Fair Oaks, and The Foundation of California State University, Sacramento. Prepared for the U.S. Army Corps of Engineers, Sacramento.

Berge, Dale L.
   1980   Simpson Springs Station, Historical Archaeology in Western Utah. Bureau of Land Management Cultural Resource Series No. 6. Salt Lake City.

Blandin, Evelyn R.
   1971   The Igo Schoolhouse. The Covered Wagon. The Shasta County Historical Society Yearbook, pp. 60-65. Redding.

Blanford, John
   1986   Bottles and Ethnicity at Riverside's Chinatown. Paper presented at the Society for Historic Archaeology Meeting, West Sacramento.

Brott, Clark W.
   1982   Moon Lee One: Life in Old Chinatown Weaverville, California. Great Basin Foundation, San Diego.

Butler Brothers
   1915   The Grocers Catalogue. Chicago.

California State Mining Bureau
   1892   Report of the State Mineralogist. California State Printing Office, Sacramento.

California State Mining Bureau
1894   Twelfth   Report   of   the   State   Mineralogist.   California
            State Printing Office, Sacramento.

California State Mining Bureau
1896   Thirteenth Report of   the   State   Mineralogist.   California
            State Printing Office, Sacramento.

Chace, Paul G.
1976   Oversees Chinese Ceramics.   In The Changing Faces of Main
            Street, edited by Roberta S. Greenwood, pp.   509-530.
            Redevelopment Agency, City of San Buenaventura.

Chance, David H. and Jennifer V. Chance
1976   Kanaka   Village/Vancouver   Barracks.   Office   of Public
            Archaeology, Institute for Environmental Studies, Reports
            in Highway Archaeology No. 3. University of Washington,
            Seattle.

Chiu, Ping
1963   Chinese   Labor   in   California,   1850-1880,   An   Economic
            Study.   The   State   Historical   Society   of   Wisconsin.
            Madison.

Clark, Hyla M.
1977   The Tin Can Book. New American Library, New York.

Clark, William B.
1963   Gold Districts of California.   California Division   of
            Mines and Geology, Bulletin No. 193. Sacramento.

DuFault, David V.
1959   The   Chinese   in   the   Mining   Camps   of   California:
            1848-1870.   Historical   Society   of   Southern   California
            Quarterly 41 (2): 155-171.

Evans, William S. Jr.
1980   Food and Fantasy: Material Culture of the Chinese in
            California   and   the   West,   Circa   1850-1900.   In
            Archaeological Perspectives on Ethnicity in America,
            edited by Robert L. Schuyler, pp. 89-97. Baywood
            Publishing Company, Inc., Farmingdale, New York.

Felton, David L., Frank Lortie, and Peter D. Schulz
1984   The Chinese Laundry on Second Street: Papers on
            Archaeology at the Woodland Opera House Site. California
            Archaeological Reports No. 24.   Department of Parks and
            Recreation, Sacramento.

Felton, David L., Bonnie S. Porter and Philip W. Hines
1979   Survey of Cultural Resources at Malakoff Diggins State
            Historic Park.   Department of Parks and Recreation,
            Sacramento.

Ferraro, Pat and Bob Ferraro
  1965   Min Gei. The Antiques Journal, pp. 20-29.
(August)

Fike, Richard E. and H. Blaine Phillips II.
  1984   A Nineteenth Century Ute Burial from Northeast Utah.
            Bureau of Land Management Cultural Resources Series No.
            16. Salt Lake City.

Fleming, J. Arnold
  1923   Scottish Pottery. Maclehose, Jackson and Company, Glasgow.

Fontana, Bernard L.
  1965   The Tale of a Nail: On the Ethnological Interpretation of
            Historic Artifacts. The Florida Anthropologist, Vol. 18
            (3), Part 2, pp. 85-90.

Gates, William C., Jr. and Dana E. Ormerod
  1982   The East Liverpool Pottery District: Identification of
            Manufacturers and Marks. Historic Archaeology 16
            (1-2):1-358.

Giles, Rosena A.
  1949   Shasta County, California: A History. Biobooks, Oakland.

Godden, Geoffrey A.
  1972   Jewitt's Ceramic Art of Great Britain, 1800-1900. Arco
            Publishing Company, Inc., New York.

Greenway, Gregory
  1985   Preliminary Results of Test Excavations and Surface
            Collections Conducted at two Rural Chinese Placer Mining
            Sites in Butte County, California. Paper presented at the
            Annual Society for California Archaeology Meeting, San
            Diego.

Greenwood, Roberta S.
  1980   The Chinese on Main Street. In Archaeological
            Perspectives on Ethnicity in America, edited by Robert L.
            Schuyler, pp. 113-124. Baywood Publishing Company, Inc.,
            Farmingdale, New York.

  1982   New Melones Archaeological Project, California: Data
            Recovery from Historic Sites. Final Report of the New
            Melones Archaeological Project, Vol. 5. Report on File
            with the National Park Service, Washington D.C.

Hamilton, Jennifer and Val Hall
  1982   Ceramics Artifact Class. In Artifact Analysis Manual for
            Historic Archaeology, Parks Canada, Prairie Region,
            Archaeology Division, edited by Dana-Mae C. Grainger
            (unpaginated). Winnipeg.

Hammond, John H.
  1890   The Auriferous Gravels of California. In Ninth Annual
            Report of the State Mineralogist, California State Mining
            Bureau. State Printing Office, Sacramento.

Hanover, Rita
  1982   The Chinese of Trinity County, An Archival History. In
            Moon Lee One: Life in Old Chinatown Weaverville,
            California by Clark W. Brott, pp. 9-29. Great Basin
            Foundation, San Diego.

Hardesty, Donald L. and Eugene M. Hattori
  1983   An Archaeological Model of Victorianism on the Nevada
            Mining Frontier. Paper presented at the Annual Society
            for Historic Archaeology Meeting, Denver.

  1984   Rural Chinese on the Nevada Mining Frontier:
            Archaeological and Historical Perspectives. Paper
            presented at the Annual Society for Historic Archaeology
            Meeting, Williamsburg.

Hull, Deborah A.
  1981   Euro-American Manufactured Remains from Walpi. Walpi
            Archaeological Project - Phase II, Volume II: Parts I and
            II. Museum of Northern Arizona, Flagstaff.

Jaffa, M. E.
  1901   Nutrition Investigations Among Fruitarians and Chinese at
            the California Agricultural Experiment Station,
            1899-1901. U.S. Department of Agriculture, Office of
            Experiment Stations, Bulletin No. 107: 1-43. Washington
            D.C.

Johnson, Jerald J. and Dorothea J. Theodoratus
  1984   Dutch Gulch Lake Intensive Cultural Resources Survey.
            Report of file with the U.S. Army Corps of Engineers,
            Sacramento.

Jones, May
  1966   The Bottle Trail. Vol. 6, Southwest Offset, Inc.,
            Hereford, Texas.

Jones, Olive
  1971   Some Comments on the Newman Dating Key. Society for
            Historical Archaeology Newsletter, Vol. 4 (3): 7-13.

Keen, Sharon
  1982   Metal Containers Artifact Class. In Artifact Analysis
            Manual for Historic Archaeology, Prairie Region,
            Archaeology Division, edited by Dana-Mae C. Grainger
            (unpaginated). Winnipeg.

Kelly, John L. and H. John McAleer
  1985   An Archaeological Survey, Assessment, and Recommendations
            for the Ohio Flat Mining District (CA-Tri-943), Trinity
            County, California. Report on file with Department of
            Water Resources, Red Bluff.

Kendrick, Grace
1964   The Antique Bottle Collector.   Western   Printing   and
        Publishing Company, Sparks, Nevada.

Klaseen, T. A. and D. K. Ellison
1974   Soil Survey of Shasta County Area, California. United
        States Department of Agriculture Soil Conservation Service
        and   Forest   Service.   United States Printing Office,
        Washington D.C.

LaLande, Jeffrey Max
1981   Sojourners in the Oregon Siskiyous: Adaptation and
        Acculturation of the Chinese Miners in the Applegate
        Valley, Ca. 1855-1900. M.A. Thesis on file at Oregon
        State University, Corvallis.

1985   Sojourners in Search of Gold: Hydraulic Mining Techniques
        of the Chinese on the Oregon Frontier.   Industrial
        Archaeology, 11(1):29-52.

LaLande, Jeffrey and Gary Handschug
1983   Cultural Resource Reconnaissance and Evaluation Report for
        the Flumet Timber Sale Planning Area. Report on file with
        the Rogue River National Forest, Medford.

Langenwalter, Paul E. II
1980   The Archaeology of 19th Century Chinese Subsistence at the
        Lower China Store, Madera County, California.   In
        Archaeological Perspectives on Ethnicity in America,
        edited by Robert L. Schuyler, pp. 102-113.   Baywood
        Publishing Company, Inc., Farmingdale, New York.

Lee, Rose Hum
1960   The Chinese in the United States of America. Hong Kong
        University Press, Hong Kong.

Lorrain, Dessamae
1968   An Archaeologist's Guide to Nineteenth Century American
        Glass. Historical Archaeology 2:35-44.

Olsen, John W.
1978   A Study of Chinese Ceramics Excavated in Tucson. The
        Kiva, Vol. 44 (1): 1-50. Tucson.

Praetzellis, Adrian and Mary Praetzellis
1979   The Lovelock Ceramics. Nevada State Museum Archaeological
        Services Reports 1:140-198. Carson City.

Praetzellis, Mary, Betty Rivers and Jeanette K. Schulz
1983   Ceramic Marks from Old Sacramento.   California
        Archaeological Reports No. 22. Department of Parks and
        Recreation, Sacramento.

Rock, James T.
1984   Cans in the Countryside. Historical Archaeology, 18(2):
        97-112.

Rusco, Mary K. and Eugene M. Hattori
   1986   Ethnic   Diversity   Among   the   Lovelock   Chinese   from
             Archaeological and Local Historical Data.   Paper presented
             at the Society for Historic Archaeology Meeting, West
             Sacramento.

Russell, Carl P.
   1967   Firearms, Traps and Tools of the Mountain Men. Alfred A.
             Knoff, New York.

Sando, Ruth Ann and David L. Felton
   1984   Inventory Records of Ceramics and Opium from a Nineteenth
             Century   Overseas   Chinese   Store.   Paper Presented at the
             Annual Society for California Archaeology Meeting, Salinas.

The Searchlight
   1898   Northern   California   Illustrated   Mining   Edition   4(10),
             February 22. Redding.

Seldner, Dana McGowan
   1986   Archival   Research   in   the   Study   of   Chinese   and
             Euro-American   Mining   in   Rural   North-Central   California.
             Paper presented at the   Society   for   Historic   Archaeology
             Meeting, West Sacramento.

Seward, George F.
   1881   Chinese   Immigration   in   its Social and Economical Aspects.
             Charles Scribner and Sons, New York.

Shay, Frank (compiler)
   1876   Chinese   Immigration: The   Social,   Moral   and   Political
             Effect   (Testimony   Taken   Before   a Committee of the Senate
             of   the   State   of   California).   State   Printing   Office,
             Sacramento.

Smith, Mary Hilderman
   1983   Chinese   Placer   Mining and Site Formation Processes.   Paper
             presented at the Annual Society for   California   Archaeology
             Meeting, San Diego.

Teague, George A. and Lynette O. Shenk
   1977   Excavations   at   Harmony   Borax   Works.   Western
             Archaeological Center Publications   in   Anthropology   No.   6
             Tucson.

Tordoff, Judith D.
   1986   Out   of   the   Mainstream: Chinese   Placer   Mining   and
             Cottonwood   Creek.   Paper   presented   at   the   Society   for
             Historic Archaeology Meeting, West Sacramento.

Tordoff, Judith D. and Mary L. Maniery
   1986   Analysis, Evaluation, Effect Determination and Mitigation
             Plan   for   Two   Chinese   Mining   Sites   in   Butte   County,
             California.   Report   on   file   with   the   Lassen   National
             Forest, Susanville.

Toulouse, Julian Harrison
  1971   Bottle Makers and Their Marks. Thomas Nelson, Inc., New
           York.

Wegars, Priscilla
  1981   Chinese Ceramics from the Vanole Site, Ouray, Colorado.
           Laboratory of Anthropology, University of Idaho, Letter
           Report 81-4. Moscow.

Woolfenden, Wallace B.
  1970   A Study in Historic Sites Archaeology.   M.A.   Thesis,
           California State University, San Francisco.

FIGURE 16

a. View east of the reservoir area and berm (CA-Sha-1512).

b. View southeasterly of reservoir area, berm and outlet
    (CA-Sha-1512).

c. View north of reservoir outlet looking into reservoir
    (CA-Sha-1512).

FIGURE 16

a

b

c

FIGURE 17

a. Feeder ditch to reservoir at CA-Sha-1512. View North.

b. Cobble and dirt plug within reservoir berm at CA-Sha-1512.

c. View southeast of hydraulically mined bluff at CA-Sha-1512.

FIGURE 17

a

b

c

FIGURE 18

a. Rock feature at Chinese camp (CA-Sha-1512). Possible hearth or structure foundation (unexcavated).

b. Main dump area at CA-Sha-1512 in background. Low cobble alignment in foreground of photo.

c. Old wagon road from Igo to reservoir area at CA-Sha-1512. View south.

FIGURE 18

APPENDIX 1

Historic Plats of Site Area
(T. 31 N., R. 6 W., SW1/4, Section 34)

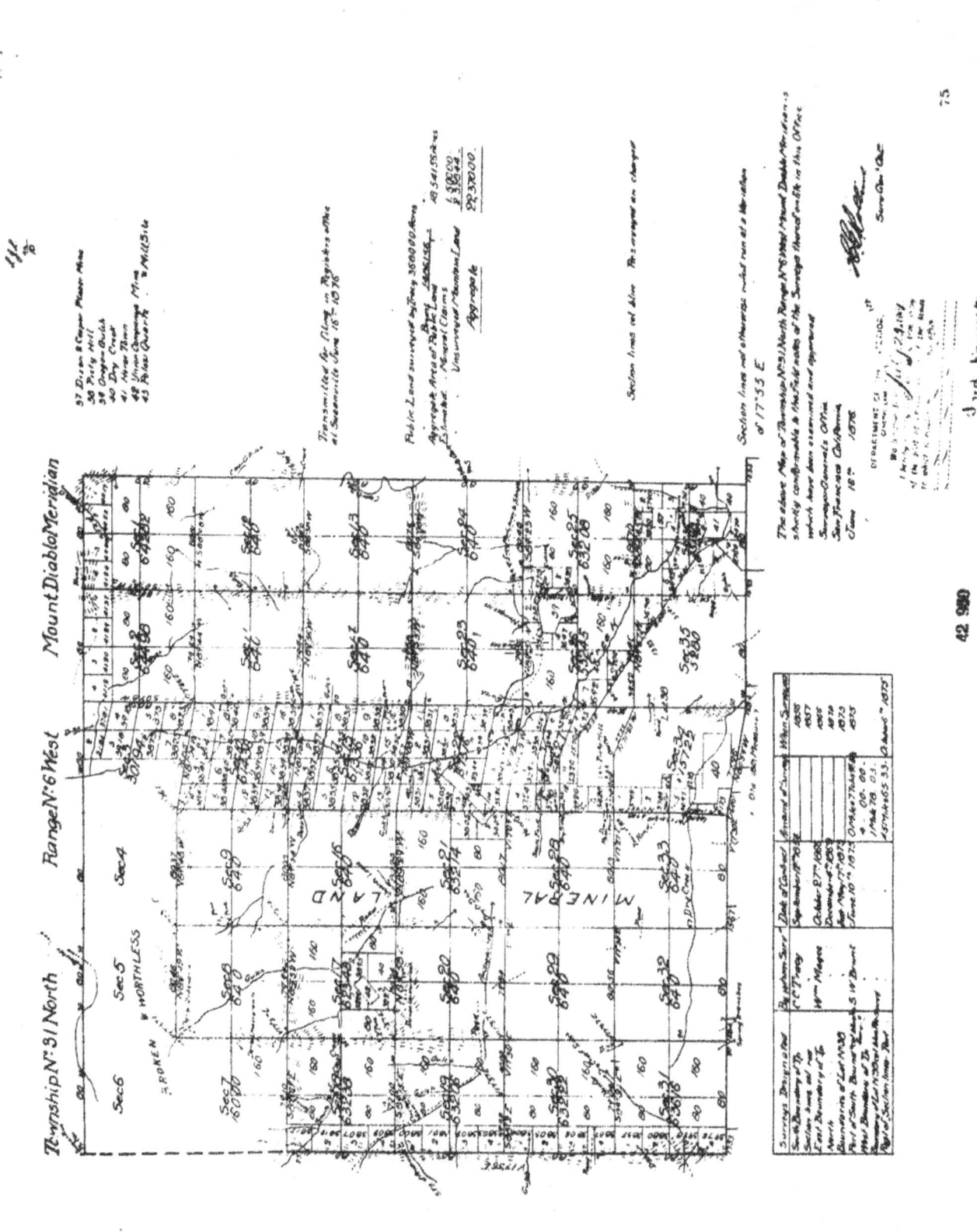

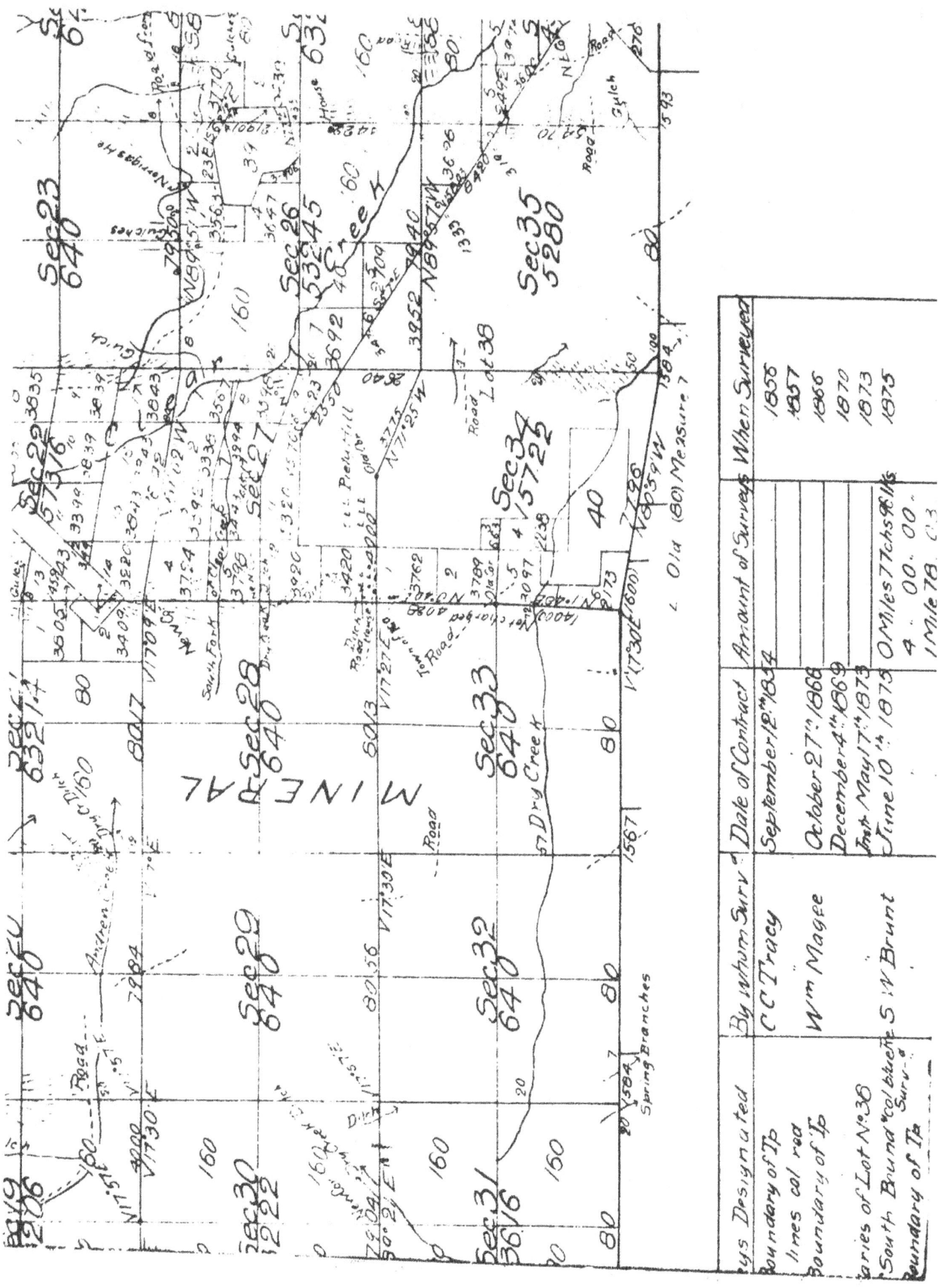

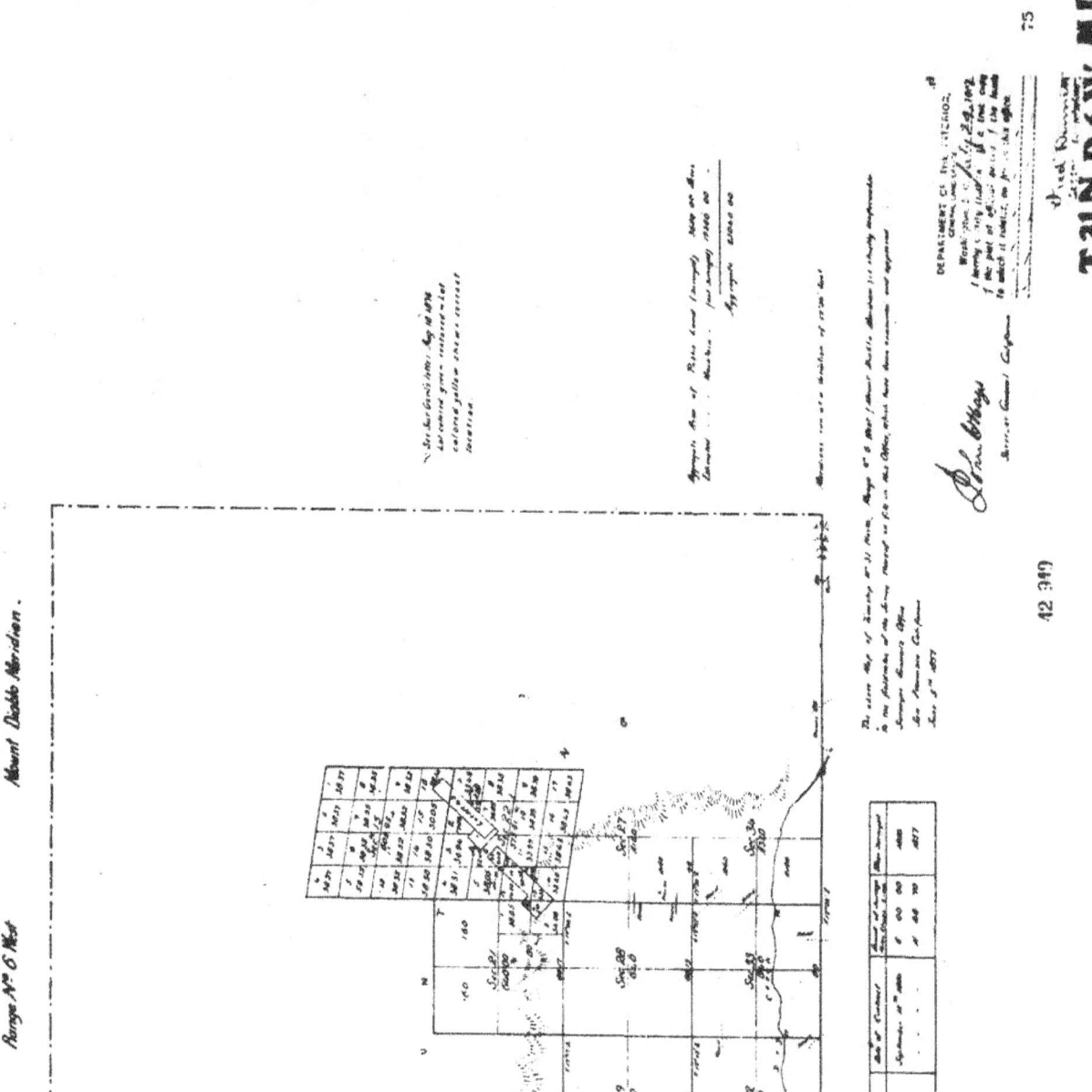

T31N R6W MD

104

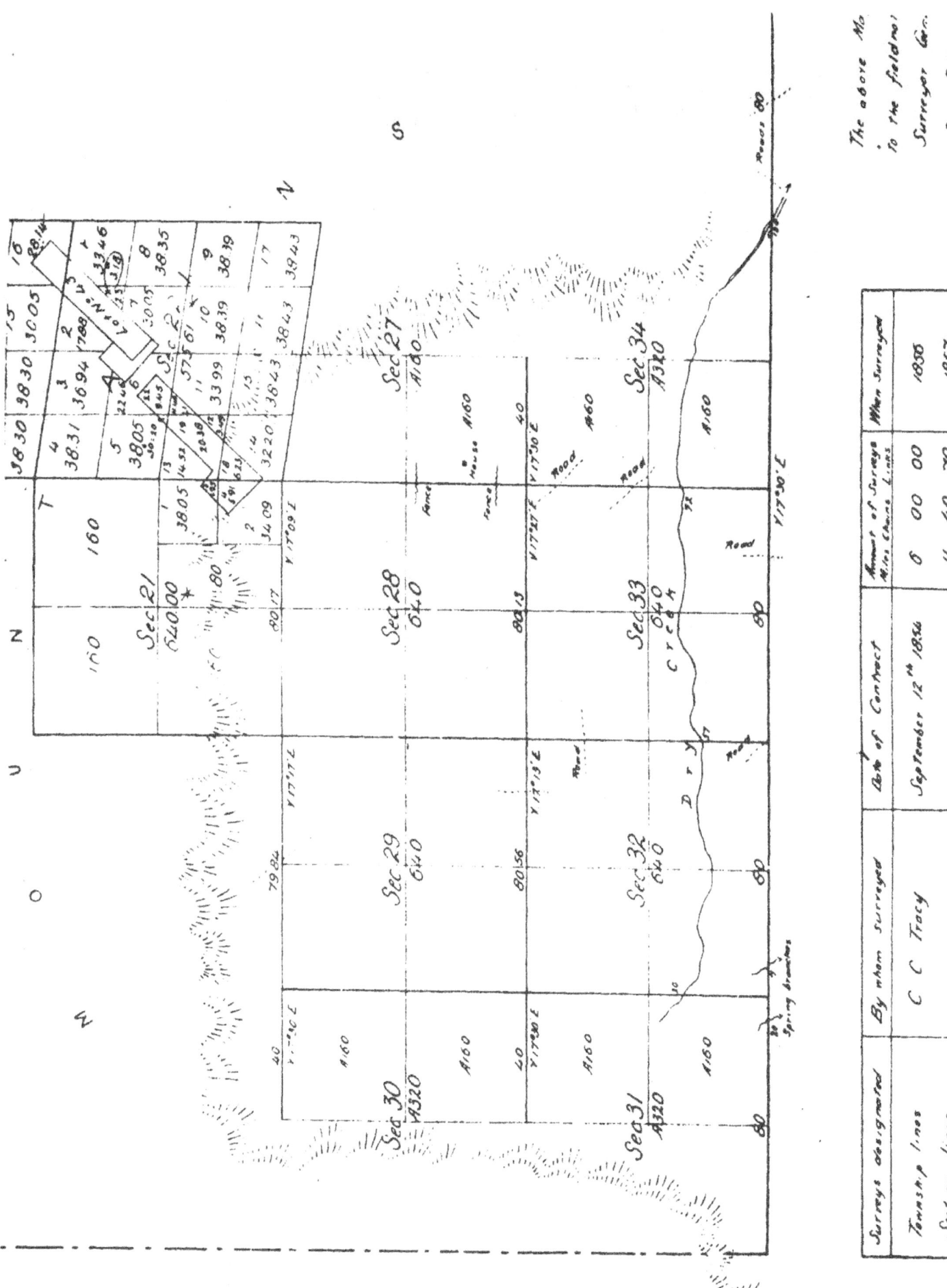

Surveys designated	By whom surveyed	Date of Contract	Amount of Surveys Miles Chains Links			When Surveyed
Township lines	C C Tracy	September 12th 1856	6	00	00	1856
Section lines	" "	" " "	11	40	70	1857

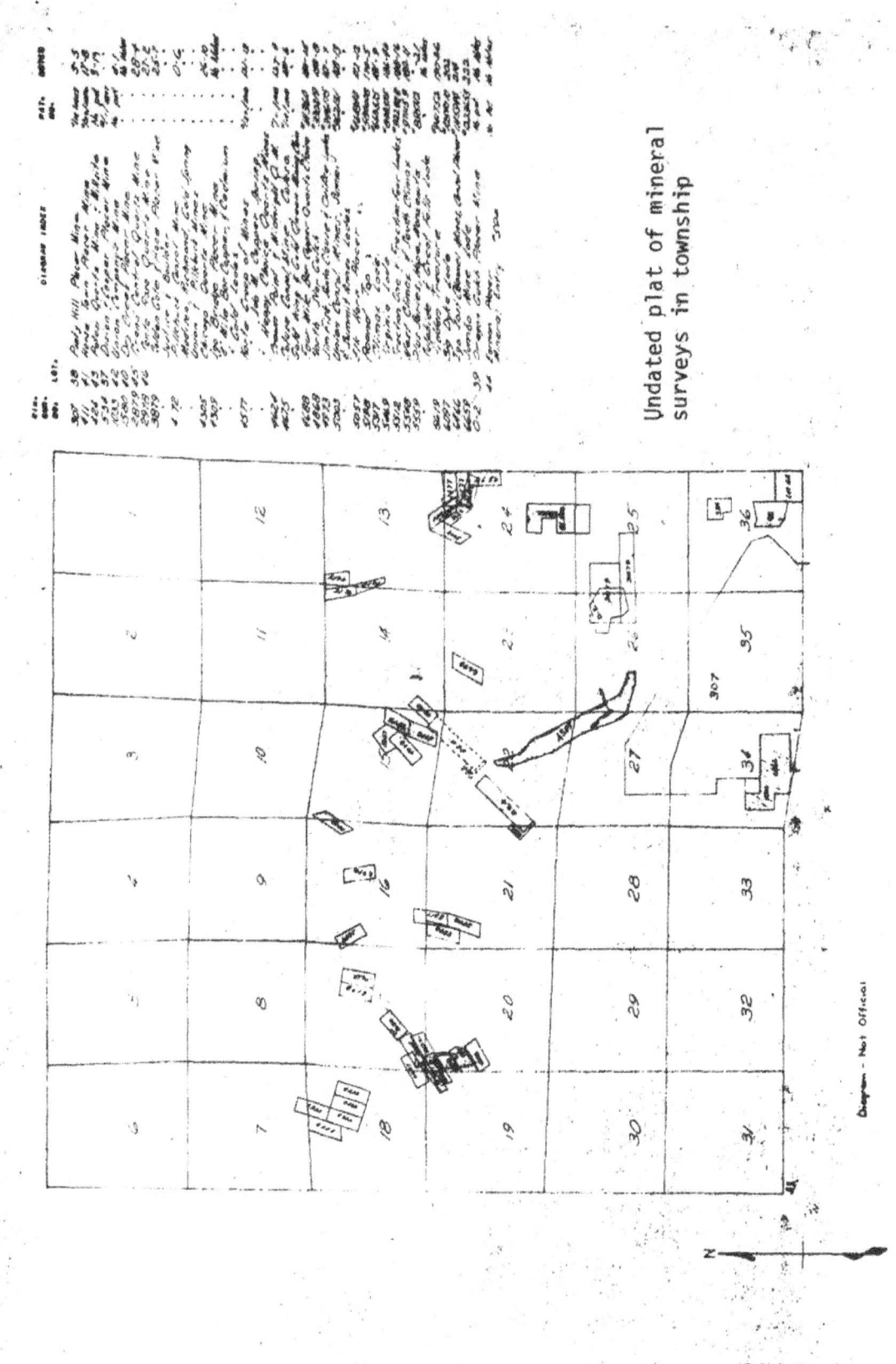

Undated plat of mineral
surveys in township

T.3I N., R.6 W., M.D.M.

42 954

Diagram - Not Official

N

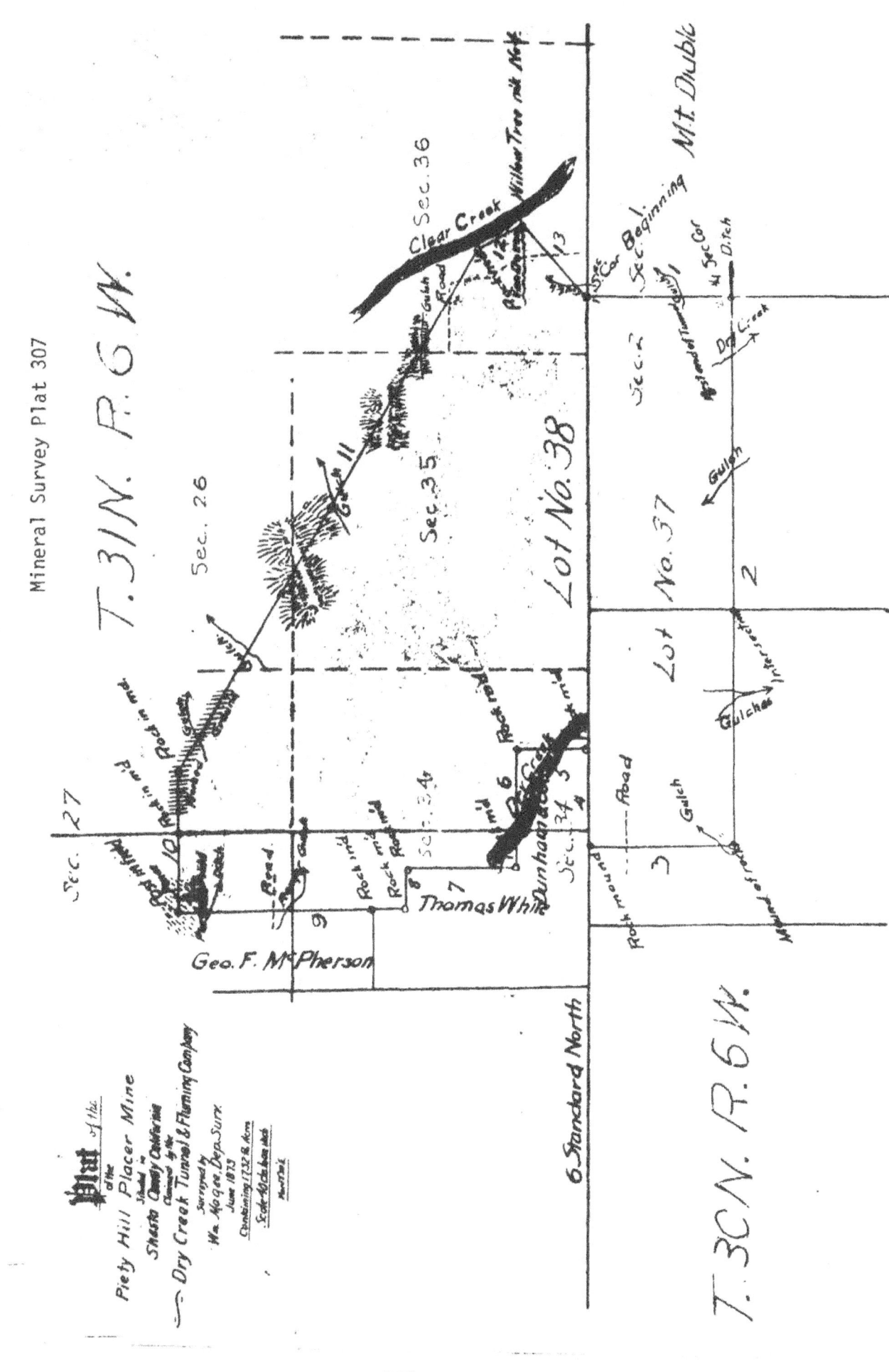

APPENDIX 2

Chinese Character Translation Notes

TRANSLATION NOTES   Chinese Comparative Collection, Laboratory of Anthropology, University of Idaho, Moscow

Catalogue No(s).: WCC 64

Location: CCC

Bay 22 Drawer 5

Description: Dark grey/grey stoneware
opium pipe bowl

Chinese Characters:

Transliteration
Pin-Yin

Zheng

Meng Bian Mu

Fu   Fu

Ji Er Ji

Wade-Giles

Chêng

Meng Pien Mu

Fu   Fu

Chi Êrh Chi

Translation:
(Mandarin or Cantonese; circle 1)

Surname

sprout side wood

Prosperity   prosperity

store   ear   store

Comment: characters stamped in base.

Descriptive translation: Fu Ji is probably the name of the store and Zheng should be the last name of the owner. I don't really know exactly what "wood's a sprout" stands for. The two round symbols are money marks.

Other references:

Translator: Joe & David Peters   Date: 4-24-83

109

TRANSLATION NOTES   Chinese Comparative Collection, Laboratory of Anthropology, University of Idaho, Moscow

Catalogue No(s).: WCC 57   Location: CCC
                                                               Bay 22 Drawer 5
Description: Red earthenware opium
             pipe bowl

Chinese Characters: Translation:
                                                 (Mandarin or Cantonese; circle 1)

Transliteration Pin-Yin			Wade-Giles		

Hua   Xing Si Yi   Hua   Hsing Ssŭ I
Hua   Hua

                                                 吉利 Color one

                                                 flower
                                                 flower

Comments: 4 characters incised on bottom.

Descriptive translation: Common Chinese script describing the object below.

Other references:

Translator: Joe & Jin Jeffern   Date: 4-23-83

110

TRANSLATION NOTES   Chinese Comparative Collection, Laboratory of Anthropology, University of Idaho, Moscow.

Catalogue No(s).:   Location: BLM, Redding, CA.
                                                            Igo site

Description of Artifact: Opium pipe bowl fragment, orange

Description of Mark: Incised Chinese characters

Transcription (in Chinese characters):

花

一 蜀
  香

Transliteration (please check):
_____ Mandarin or _____ Cantonese
_____ Pinyin   _____ Wade-Giles

huā   Yī
           Sè
           īng

Translation (please check):
←——— or ———→

flower   ?

color

orange

Descriptive translation: _____

Other references:

Comments:

Translator: _____   Date: 7-23-96

111